YOUTH UNEMPLOYMENT AND THE FAMILY

This book examines an area of social life which has not been investigated widely: the relationship between parents and young adults living in the parental home. Tracing the effects of a poor labour market on 40 families in the North-East, the book reveals how change in the public domain of the economy penetrates the routines and intimacies of family life.

The text gives voice to those affected, particularly to parents, who are seldom heard, revealing the continuing importance of the family in times of stress and its role in the mediation of social change.

As well as social change, the theme of social order runs through the book: the pursuit of order and predictability through which people try to make sense of their lives, the resources out of which such order is constructed (time, space and economic, social, cultural and emotional capital), and the essential fragility of the order created.

The book is essential reading for anyone interested in the price paid for the economic restructuring of Britain that has been underway since the 1970s and challenges the notion that unemployment is more easily borne by those living in regions where it has been endemic.

The book will be of interest to students of youth, unemployment and social policy as well as those involved in vocational training. It should also appeal to anyone interested in the present day working-class family and working-class culture.

'Allatt and Yeandle's book is a fine example of contemporary ethnographic research which balances attention to detail about values, emotions and actions with the social anthropologist's skill and interest in broader theoretical issues. The authors explain more vividly and convincingly than any other text how persistent unemployment erodes the social and moral fabric of private life'

Professor Ken Roberts, Liverpool University

Patricia Allatt is a Reader at Teesside Business School, Teesside Polytechnic; **Susan Yeandle** is a Senior Lecturer in Sociology and Social Policy at the Department of Applied Social Sciences, Nottingham Polytechnic.

YOUTH UNEMPLOYMENT AND THE FAMILY

Voices of disordered times

Patricia Allatt and Susan Yeandle

London and New York

First published in 1992
by Routledge
11 New Fetter Lane, London EC4P 4EE

Simultaneously published in the USA and Canada
by Routledge
a division of Routledge, Chapman and Hall Inc.
29 West 35th Street, New York, NY 10001

Typeset by Selectmove Ltd, London
Printed and bound in Great Britain by
Biddles Ltd, Guildford and King's Lynn

British Library Cataloguing in Publication Data
Allatt, Patricia
Youth unemployment and the family: voices of disordered times.
1. Great Britain. Families. Effects of unemployment
I. Title II. Yeandle, Susan
306.850941

Library of Congress Cataloging in Publication Data
Allatt, Patricia.
Youth unemployment and the family: voices of disordered times
P. Allatt and S.M. Yeandle.
p. cm.
Includes bibliographical references (p.) and index.
1. Youth–Employment–Great Britain–Sociological aspects.
2. Young adults–Employment–Great Britain–Sociological aspects.
3. Unemployment–Great Britain–Sociological aspects.
4. Unemployed–Great Britain–Family relationships. I. Yeandle, Susan. II.
Title.
HD6276.G7A64 1991 91–2708
331.3'4137941–dc20 CIP

ISBN 0–415–01851–X

OR 2/93

Ref (ESF)

306.850941 ALL

X 40861

CONTENTS

TABLES AND FIGURES

TABLES

FIGURES

PREFACE

With the alarming rise in the rate of youth unemployment over the last two decades, when of those leaving school at 16 fewer and fewer have entered paid employment directly, the focus of attention has been largely upon the young unemployed themselves, particularly school-leavers, and the government training measures set up in response to the problem. The research upon which this book is based took a different approach. It brought together two fields of investigation which are usually considered separately: the family and youth unemployment. The neglect of this convergence seems strange, especially today when the family looms large in at least the rhetoric of political agendas, since the problems encountered in the labour market are literally brought home by the majority of young people. Within the family – in a young person's relationships with parents, brothers and sisters, in the routines and expectations of family life, in the deployment of resources to these ends, and where social identity has its early roots – the state of the labour market is critical.

The study looked at the families of employed and unemployed young adults who had entered the labour market at 16 – a neglected group, beyond the years of youth training provision. The study, conducted between 1983 and 1985, was made possible by the generous support of the Leverhulme Trust, and in these days of ever-tighter research budgets this support is gratefully acknowledged. Little has been written of the relationships between the generations in ordinary families, and the grant enabled the window on these everyday relationships between young people and their parents, first opened by Diana Leonard (1980) in the early 1970s, to be widened at a time when poor job opportunities highlighted their importance. Several studies have demonstrated that the effects of unemployment extend beyond the unemployed individual. Consequently, this study was designed to give both mothers and fathers, as well as young people, a voice on the effects of a poor youth labour market.

The presence of 'voices' in the title of the book is due, not quite in the way he expected, to one of the readers. His feeling of an inability to identify with the informants over the course of the book, that they were more like voices that come and go, clarified an underlying theme. The people here, in families of both employed and unemployed, led lives which were severely affected by economic change and restructuring labour markets; they were not engaged and, perhaps, could not engage in any dialogue with those with any power of amelioration. Neither could those who felt constrained to look after their own family interests, or for whom unemployment created a barrier of shame and embarrassment, create a dialogue amongst themselves. Thus a poor and fluctuating labour market not only disordered people's lives but also fragmented the expression they gave to these experiences. In any case, the direction which social and employment policies have taken with regard to young people, and the assumptions made about the family's economic and caring capacity – issues carefully analysed over the years by such bodies as Youthaid, the Unemployment Unit and the Child Poverty Action Group – suggest that even if heard, such voices or any representations made on their behalf would carry little weight.

Since the study was completed, the high rates of recorded unemployment for those aged between 18 and 24 have substantially declined, although they are now beginning to rise once more. Throughout, however, regional variation has continued and unemployment rates have remained high in the North-East; the contemporary figures have been included in Chapter One. Those who would have appeared in the younger age band have now disappeared almost entirely into the government programmes of special measures. The situation described in the book thus has a continuing relevance for a large number of people.

As well as charting aspects of economic change amongst forty families, the book has more general sociological import. Two related themes run through the book: social change and social order. Economic change affects power relationships and exposes and alters the resources, not only economic, with which people negotiate their place in the order of things both inside and outside the family. The book is also about the interpenetration of the public and private domains of social life. Change and uncertainty in the public sphere, in this case a poor youth labour market, penetrate lives and familial relationships at many levels. They intrude into social and psychological existence, ranging, for example, from the experience of the labour market itself to the use of the bathroom, the prioritization of values and the sense of well-being and of belonging in both family and society. In turn, the ensuing decisions and practices in the private sphere of the family feed into, indeed are part of, the embracing ethos of the wider society. This is true of all major change. Numerous novels trace the intimate, personal details of change arising from the interdependency of historical time and personal biography; one has only to recall Giuseppe Tomasi di Lampedusa's (1988) Prince Fabrizio in revolutionary Italy. What is attempted here is a sociological understanding.

There is no single correct way to analyse data, and the book is organized around what were seen as major themes arising from the data. To present the material in a book imposes further constraints of space; consequently the account is necessarily selective. The aim is to provide a framework for further work. For although the study is, with one exception, of white, working-class families, the variation amongst them provided material for an extensive elaboration of each theme. The theme of independence, for example, whilst taking different paths according to class, race and gender, is nonetheless a major value in our society, and the study sets out some of the parameters affected by economic change which can be pursued across social divisions at a later date. Similarly, whilst in the more recent studies of young people gender is frequently used as an analytical category, here it is used to illustrate other sociological issues, and more developed gender comparisons are left for later work or for others to take up.

Blanche Geer once wished she could 'write what she had to say on the surface of a sphere, so that nothing would come first' (Becker 1986: 59). Thus, although presented sequentially, what is described occurs concurrently. Consequently, one response sometimes illustrated several facets of a situation and, as a result, a quotation might be referred to more than once in the text. This is particularly so for Chapter Five, on values, in which it seemed important to integrate previously mentioned issues.

Parts of the book draw upon work which has already appeared. Thanks are due to the Department of Social Policy and Professional Studies, University of Hull, for permission to include in Chapter

Three material from the paper, 'The young unemployed: independence and identity' (Allatt 1986a). Much of the substance of Chapter Four was presented in 1986 at the Annual Conference of the Association for Social Studies of Time, Dartington, as 'The dis-ease of social change', and is to be published in Frankenberg (ed) *Time and Health*. Similarly, parts of Chapter Five have been published as '"It's not fair, is it?" Youth unemployment, family relations and the social contract'(Allatt and Yeandle 1986), in Allen *et al.* (eds) *The Experience of Unemployment*. The ideas about family resources, described in Chapter One, were developed out of a paper presented in 1987 in the *ESRC Resources within Households Workshop Series*, Thomas Coram Research Unit, entitled, 'In trust: young people and transfers within households'.

Thanks are due to many others: Olivia Grant, formerly Principal Careers Officer, City of Newcastle upon Tyne, and her staff; Demott Dick, County Careers Officer, Durham County Council; Geoff Norris and John Blackie, Policy Services Unit, and Ian McCalman, Housing Department, City of Newcastle upon Tyne; Margaret Curran, Tyne and Wear County-Wide Research and Intelligence Unit; Jo Richmond of the Big Lamp Project, Newcastle upon Tyne; and to all those who were consulted about the area in which the investigation took place but who cannot be named for reasons of confidentiality. A debt is also owed to those who helped to shape the ideas and methodology both before and during the research, particularly Lorna McKee and Marie Johnston, and to Bob Holland and Rowena Gaunt of Routledge for their helpful comments on completion of the draft. Thanks go to the interviewers upon whom so much depended, George English, Peter McMylor, Frank Pike and Mabel Williamson; thanks are also due for the secretarial and administrative services of Alison Bloomer and for the transcription and typing skills of Christine Cummings of Topline Secretarial and Business Services, Linda Thompson and Helen Wright. Finally, thanks go to all the respondents who gave hours of their time and who received the intrusion into their lives and their families with kindness and courtesy. All the names used in the book are, of course, fictitious.

P. Allatt
Teesside Polytechnic
S. Yeandle
Nottingham Polytechnic
1990

1

INTRODUCTION
Family, history and biography

INTRODUCTION

This book is about parents and their children in their late teens and early twenties who are still living at home. It is a study of the families of forty young adults, with various experiences of employment and unemployment, who in the early 1980s were living in one neighbourhood of Newcastle upon Tyne.

The book looks at the conjunction of two types of social change within the setting of family life. One type arises from those events and transitions that people think of as normal aspects of the life course, such as work, marriage and parenthood, and which they expect to constitute the substance of their lives. The second is societal change, in this case a restructuring labour market and high rates of youth unemployment brought about by economic and technological change.

At all times and at all ages, changes in personal lives and public arenas intersect; but in the few transitional years between the end of childhood and the entry into adulthood the effects of the conjuncture are heightened for two reasons. First, several critical decisions and events are compressed into this period, including leaving or staying on at school, entering the labour market, courtship, leaving home and marriage. This is not to suggest that these events are smooth, discrete or irreversible. Leaving home, for example, may be a ragged process of leaving and returning for a variety of reasons, such as entry into higher education, periods of employment away from home, experimental independence, or trial partnerships or marriages which break down. Nonetheless, change in the labour market can disrupt or enhance both the quality and the progress of personal journeys through life. Second, during the interstitial

1

state between dependence and independence most young people live with their parents. Although official statistics cannot reveal the patterns of leaving and returning to the parental home before final departure is made, Kiernan's (1985) analysis of the 1980 census data shows that a large proportion of young people were still living at home at the age of 21 – 43 per cent of women and 63 per cent of men. When paid employment, the symbol of and stepping stone to independence and adulthood, is scarce and uncertain, the management of processes which shape the anticipated and expected independence becomes problematic.

Paradoxically, the family can both inhibit and facilitate social change. Land observed that, as the key institution that transmits a culture to the next generation, the family can be 'a powerful force for the transmission of the status quo', yet the family also 'manages, or is expected to manage, the tensions between order and change' (Land 1979: 14). The paradox is at the heart of some of the problems and dilemmas which families encounter. For example, historical change over a relatively short period can produce contrasts between the experience of entry into the labour market of young people today and that of their parents or even of older siblings. The lack of shared experience harbours the potential for outmoded or inappropriate advice, misunderstandings, and lack of empathy or even sympathy.

The management of social change is also set within a moral order. In a society grown accustomed to economic growth and a high standard of living, extensive unemployment can create cultural as well as structural disjunctions (Kornhauser 1960). As in war time, not only are established daily routines upset but values are challenged and contradictions in the culture exposed (Allatt 1981a). A familistic ideology, therefore, which means that in a poor labour market 'you first look after your own', competes with a general sense of what is fair.

The study thus draws out the role of the family in cultural change. This familial mediation of the intersection of personal change and societal change takes place not just through words but through the deployment of a family's resources and the transactions and negotiations which texture people's lives, especially in the interaction between the generations, parents and children. These processes, the benefits and the losses, affect not only the material aspects of life but also influence how people perceive and interpret their world. This implies a duality. Morgan (1985) has noted the Janus–faced nature of the family, looking both towards the individual and towards society. Thus how family members deal with personal change in a harsh economic climate contributes in turn to the surrounding environment of wider societal changes. The book, therefore, is also concerned with how the mediation of this coincidence of change within the structure of family relationships – that is, in the micro-culture of the family – impinges upon the wider society.

FAMILY RESOURCES AND FAMILY RELATIONSHIPS

In considering the coincidence of personal and societal change, the book also brings together two areas of social concern that are usually considered separately: the family and the youth labour market, particularly youth unemployment. Traditionally, ranging from theoretical to common-sense understandings, the two have been seen and treated as belonging to distinct and separate domains, the public and the private; and the problems of youth unemployment have largely been conceptualized as residing in the public domain of economic and social relationships or seen as problems for the individual.

Thus in both journalistic accounts and research the major focus of interest in youth unemployment has been on issues and institutions outside the family. For example, comments and accounts in the press and other media, as well as general public opinion, have linked both increasing crime and vandalism and such self-destructive deviancy as solvent abuse with the growing number of unemployed young people. And as Taylor observed in the early 1980s, 'The prospect of so many idle youngsters on the streets of Britain worries the Department of Employment (and, no doubt, the Home Office also)' (Taylor 1982: 308).

This perspective has been accompanied by an awareness of the political aspects of a problem which also arose during the mass unemployment of the 1930s (Morgan 1939): the phenomenon of the youthful unemployed who might never work. This group is seen as the bearer of a potential threat to the social order arising from the opposing conceptualizations of an increasingly apathetic mass ripe for political manipulation (Kornhauser 1960) or, alternatively, from an increased political consciousness amongst the out-of-work young. The public disorder of the inner cities during the summer of 1981 correctly or incorrectly served to raise this spectre.

3

Furthermore, where the private sphere has been addressed, the particular emphasis placed upon the individual has focused interest and research upon the social and psychological effects of unemployment upon the young themselves; on, for example, the crisis of identity (Breakwell 1984), perceptions of unemployment (Kelvin and Jarrett 1985; Ullah 1987), dilemmas posed by a traditional work ethic (Selbourne 1982) and strategies of adaptation and coping (Coffield *et al.* 1983).[1]

Both theoretically and empirically, however, the omission of the interpenetration of public and private worlds is surprising, since a person's experience in the labour market and the effects of the changes occurring there are literally 'brought home'. Uncertainty, loss of earnings, and the likelihood of increased dependency upon parental support are accompanied by the actual physical presence of the young person in the home. The combination directly raises the question of the family's response to a difficult labour market, particularly to the unemployment of its young, and the impact of possibly long-term unemployment upon family relationships. This in turn raises questions about access to and use of individual and family resources.

Historical and contemporary evidence suggests that the family is an important resource characterized by its flexibility. It forms the bulwark against those 'critical life situations' enumerated by Anderson (1981) – old age, sickness, death and unemployment – even in a society which, unlike the nineteenth-century Lancashire which he examined, has an infrastructure of bureaucratic provision. In the economic climate of the early 1980s there was already evidence that, although the incidence may have fallen unevenly upon family members, families had for some time been absorbing the costs of a changing society. Families were compensating as best they could for the reduction in public services attendant upon inflation and government economies (Counter Information Services 1976), and some parents were lowering expectations for themselves if not, initially, for their children (Unemployment Unit Bulletin 1981).

Costs could also be carried by families when unemployment or low rate of pay deterred a young person from leaving home. It is a situation which is further complicated by social policies directed towards the young.[2] The board and lodging regulations, the community charge and the reduction (from April 1988) of social security benefits for those under 25 years of age, for example, while engendering different responses according to family resources, nonetheless have extensive ramifications for family economic relationships. Thus while in some cases parents may be able to provide loans and gifts which enable their children to live independently (Allatt 1988a), in others young people may be obliged to remain in the parental home, dependent upon and sharing familial resources which cannot be stretched to provide aid beyond the confines of the household. Alternatively, the response may echo the domestic strategy noted by Holley (1981, cited in Pahl 1984: 66) in his description of two types of family economies in Victorian Scotland: 'poor families shed their children when the economies of unemployment dictated'. It is a position which, for example, changes in housing benefit have thrust upon some parents today (Cusack and Roll 1985). Moreover, while in the 1930s Newcastle was an 'exporter', both formally and informally, of adult and juvenile labour (Pilgrim Trust 1938; Morgan 1939), in the early 1980s extensive emigration was limited not only by a low national demand for labour but also by the high cost of accommodation in more prosperous regions, thus further enforcing young people's dependence upon the parental home. Indeed the attempt to find work elsewhere can merely serve to increase homelessness (Guardian 1982).

The changes in the labour market and the deployment of family resources, therefore, have implications for the nature of family relationships. Anderson (1971) noted the connection between young people's greater economic independence in a thriving nineteenth-century economy and the quality of normative, affective and instrumental relationships between parents and children. There is, however, little contemporary data on the position of the economically active young within the field of negotiated familial relationships and, when the Newcastle study started,[3] none on the impact of a child's unemployment – although Leonard's (1980) point about the costs which may be incurred and Rimmer's (n.d.) evidence that when a father is unemployed the economic contribution of employed children raises the family income to a greater extent than that of an employed wife suggest that youth unemployment may have major economic consequences for some families.

While the stage between leaving school and entering marriage has been defined as one of social homelessness, for most young people in our society this is located physically and, for the most part, amicably within the family of origin (Department of Education and Science 1983; Leonard 1980; Longfield 1984; Schofield 1965). Most studies of relations between parents and young people, however, have been set within a framework of the innate individual development of the child and its striving for independence; and factors such as the stage in the family life cycle of the parents – the looming trauma of the 'empty nest' stage for the mother and the reassessment of career prospects by the middle-aged (middle-class) father – have been seen as contaminating the analysis (Conger 1973: 218–21). Alternatively, these familial relationships have been studied as pathological responses within a closed and destructive familial system (Griffin 1987; and see Morgan's (1975) discussion of the work of Laing and Cooper, especially Chapter Four).

A different approach to the study of family relationships is adopted by Leonard (1980) in her study of courtship and marriage in South Wales in which she develops the concept of the political economy of parenthood. Drawing upon Blau's (1964) propositions and Anderson's (1971) elaboration of exchange theory, Leonard counters the widespread belief in Britain that adolescence is a period inevitably marked by rebelliousness and friction with all authorities – be they parents, school, university or police – as young people struggle for independence. This struggle, in which it is often suggested young people find parents and kin particularly oppressive, is often presented as the struggle of individuals for self-determination and expression. Leonard (1980), however, prefers to define the struggle as one between age classes for power. Thus the transition of the individual to adulthood is partly a transition in family relationships as the balance of power changes.

This approach allows a series of questions to be raised about resources and power: their availability to different members of a family, how they are affected by a poor labour market, how they are distributed and used, and the interplay amongst them at this transitional stage in the life courses of both the individual and the family as a group. At this period in their lives, by virtue of age and income, young people expect to have new resources at their disposal which promise increased independence and power in its negotiation. A depressed labour market restricts the economic independence of the young adult, raising questions about the role of paid employment in the transition to full adulthood and about the exchanges and transactions amongst family members which shape and signify independence and, ultimately, full citizenship.

Resources are not solely economic. As Komarovsky (1971) showed in her study of the familial authority of unemployed men, resources may include a loving relationship as well as those resources embedded in relationships with kin, community and formal institutions. Thus, questions concerning power, authority, control and exploitation, and the allocation of resources and costs can be explored within a context of normative, affective and instrumental relationships: what people expect of each other, how much they care about each other and how much they exploit or utilize each other.

Although more prominent in some chapters than others, the notion of resources is a thread which runs through the book, shaped to the themes of the different chapters. It is useful, therefore, to briefly outline some of the dimensions which have been important to the interpretation of the data. Although the list could be extended, the resources which seemed to be particularly prominent in the Newcastle study were those of time and space, domestic labour or service, and the four forms of capital: economic, social, cultural and emotional (Bourdieu 1971; Nowotny 1981; Wallman 1984). The terminology of the economist evokes a rich vocabulary of exchange with connotations of power and differential access. Resources, whatever they are, can for example, be accumulated, wasted, bartered, invested, given, lent, borrowed and repaid with interest. Family members may resort to bribery or emotional blackmail. One kind of resource can be converted into another, or a resource may lose its currency. Collectively such transfers and transactions constitute the give and take of family life.

Resources are not simple entities. They are complex in themselves, some more so than others, are complexly interrelated, and carry complex connotations which penetrate our social and moral being. All these resources are deeply affected by the condition of the labour market. As Wallman (1984) noted in her study of households as resource systems, time is a special resource which can show remarkable shifts in value, in some circumstances becoming more of a burden than an asset, a characteristic clearly demonstrated in studies of unemployment, such as Jahoda *et al.*'s (1972) study of Marienthal in the 1930s. We can experience time as flying or dragging, expanding or contracting, but time never stands still. Time is imbued with moralities, particularly associated with the work ethic that proclaims time is money and should not be wasted. Moreover, the regularities and sequencing of our lives provide structure, order, meaning and a sense of belonging.

In the personal journey through life, time and space are intimately linked. It is important to be in the right place at the right time, whether this is in a home of one's own or being out of bed at the 'right' time; living space can be critical when unemployment strikes one or more members of a family, or when adult children show no sign of leaving the parental home. Moreover, rights accrue to those in the right place. Rights to space at specific times – for example, use of the bathroom – are linked to labour market roles.

Certain costs of resources become evident at this transitional stage of a young person's life. Domestic labour, particularly a mother's services, literally enters the reckoning when children enter the labour market. Although the full cost is not usually covered, the cost of living is nonetheless made visible through young people's contribution to household expenses in the form of board money and the discussion which surrounds it.

Capital, as an embracing concept, refers to the accumulation of resources which can be used reproductively. In this study economic capital is taken to mean the accumulation of wealth and the money and goods which enter the household from whatever source. It is this resource which is most immediately affected by a poor labour market. The reproductive element of capital, however, in the sense of its use in the creation of, or as a gateway to, other resources is wider than the economic.

The concept of social capital (Bourdieu 1971) has been employed in many studies. Nowotny summarizes this as 'social knowledge, contacts, privileged access to culturally valued qualifications and social skills as embodied in the various strategies employed by competitors in the social field (a network of power relations characterized by its own rules of competition, conflicts and strategies and interests and profits)' (Nowotny 1981: 147–8).

Social capital can be a valuable asset in the job market but is itself affected by the condition of that market. In the North-East, the declining traditional industrial base is eroding the social capital of the skilled working-class male, witnessed in the dramatic reduction of prized apprenticeships (Ashton and Maguire, n.d.); although a father may still speak for his son, there are fewer jobs to speak for. The father may, moreover, have lost his own place in the labour market and thus access to valuable social networks.

In some respects distinctions between social and cultural capital are difficult to make (Fitz and Hood-Williams 1981). For practical purposes, however, cultural capital can be taken to include educational qualifications and general culture, along with a resource that Wallman (1984) refers to as identity (in her study, ethnic identity). Families and individuals build up reputations for respectability and for having 'proper' attitudes towards work; such reputations become increasingly important for obtaining work if informal recruiting methods are used by employers. Such identities clearly fall within the domain of cultural capital or symbolic property (Allen 1982, cited in Leiulfsrud and Woodward 1987). But the connection between social and cultural capital is implicit in Harris' (1985) emphasis on the importance of prior social networks at times when competition for jobs is fierce; for reputations to count, channels must exist for knowledge of the reputations to reach those with the power to offer jobs.

Emotional capital is particularly pertinent to a study of familial processes. It is similar to social capital but differs in that it can only be used within the bounds of affective relationships. According to Nowotny, emotional capital comprises

> knowledge, contacts and relationships, as well as access to emotionally valued skills and assets, which hold within any social network characterized by affective ties. . . . Like other forms of capital it can be accumulated so that holders build up positions of dominance – but their reach only extends as far as the validity of this currency: it is limited to the private sphere. The rules of the labour market are such that emotional capital gained in the private sphere is not convertible into *economic capital* since this exchange relationship has been depersonalized, and private capital is of little value in the outside world (emphasis in original).
>
> (Nowotny 1981: 148)

Emotional capital, valueless in the public sphere, is thus largely used for family investment, especially by women, in husbands and children. The education of mothers, for example, is seen as a valuable asset for children's advancement, and mothers' economic capital gained in the labour market is converted into emotional capital, by, for example, devoting it to household expenditure rather than to themselves (Lister and Wilson 1976; Nowotny 1981).

Despite this emphasis, however, emotional capital is not confined to women. Both men and children have access to it, for the concept can be extended to include love and affection. By the time young adulthood is reached, many children will have accumulated a great deal of this resource. The first instalment of such capital originates in the mere fact that they are their parents' children. Whilst recognizing that this is not true in all cases, as instances of child abuse attest, and that the way in which a relationship develops between the growing child and the parent(s) must influence the limits and quality of this bond, nonetheless there can be large reserves of love and affection upon which even wayward children can draw. The following comment by one mother in the Newcastle study illustrates how birth, literally, gave this resource to a child; it also indicates the power into which the child can convert it. 'When I had her, I just think there was nobody like her. . . . I was just sort of very possessive. And her dad's the same with her. She can get away with *murder* off him. She's always that bit special' (Mrs Davis) (emphasis in original).

In sum, then, the approach opened up by Leonard (1980) directs attention to types of family resources, their vulnerability and limitations, and how they are exploited as life courses and societal changes are negotiated through family relationships. The language of exchange also directs attention to some of the metaphors through which people describe their lives and, by extension, how life is perceived and understood.

A familial focus which draws attention to resources is important for another reason: it is a means of challenging ways of conceptualizing those who are unemployed. Studies are now appearing which emphasize the roots of unemployment which lie outside the individual. They demonstrate, for example, that the unemployed are a heterogeneous group and that unemployment arises from structural shifts in a labour market where the demand for existing skills has disappeared (White 1983), or emphasize the overwhelming effect of recession upon the supply of jobs (Raffe 1986). Frequently, however, studies of unemployment have focused on the characteristics of unemployed people themselves, claiming that in comparison with those in work the unemployed tend to have fewer qualifications and are more likely to come from large families, often cared for by one parent. If from two-parent families, it is suggested, other members are likely to be unemployed or the family is likely to be dependent upon unemployment benefit or supplementary allowances (Carroll 1979). The National Youth Employment Council (1970, cited by Carroll 1979:8) reported that 48.5 per cent of the young unemployed who were registered at ninety-one randomly selected careers offices over a three-week period had such family backgrounds.

Some of these relationships, however, may be spurious. They can also be misleading in that they are liable to be construed as social characteristics of the individual rather than as indicators of the patterns of social relationships (including labour market relationships) in which an individual is situated. They ignore, for example, the differences in the social capital to which an individual has access as well as the condition of the labour market. Thus it may be that living in a one-parent family, and similarly in a family where all are unemployed, substantially reduces the network of contacts that provide avenues of access to paid employment. Research into recruiting policy (Jenkins *et al.* 1983) shows that as the number of jobs declines, firms increasingly use informal methods of recruitment. The social networks, implicit here, are pathways for the conversion of social and cultural capital into economic capital. It is essential, therefore, that not only are people linked into the labour market, but that the link is appropriate. A miner, for example, would be unable to speak for his daughter. As noted above, reputations by definition have to be conveyed. To be respectable and hard-working is to no avail in the labour market if such qualities are not fed through those channels which Elias and Scotson have referred to in another context as the 'gossip mills' (Elias and Scotson 1965). These considerations of social structure and culture therefore prompt questions as to whether some families are more able than others both to promote the employment careers of their children and to sustain in their children a quality of eligibility for employment.

THE CHANGING LABOUR MARKET

The families who took part in the study were affected by the kind of economic change which has now been widely commented upon: the broad change in the economy which has led to the decline of the heavy manufacturing industries and the rise of others and to the restructuring of work patterns (Cooke 1986). The families lived in the North-East of England in a working-class neighbourhood of Newcastle upon Tyne, described in Appendix One. In contrast to the Midland location selected by Bell and McKee (1982), where experience of large-scale unemployment was relatively new, the Northern Region has suffered from persistent decline since the turn of the century. Even in the years of economic growth, unemployment rates have been high relative to the rest of the country. This has been well documented elsewhere (see, for example, the North Tyneside Community Development Project (CDP) 1978). To place the study in context, however, the bones of this history are summarized here.

Up to the First World War, the Northern Region was dominated by the major heavy industries of coal mining, iron and steel, shipbuilding and heavy engineering, and their related service industries of shipping and dockwork. These industries, and the individuals who worked in them, were severely affected by the depression of the 1920s and 1930s. Later attempts to solve the employment problem by diversifying the industrial base failed. Although there has since been a further erosion of this base, writing in 1977 the CDP research team noted that the traditional industries continued to exist and, in parts of the region, continued to employ large numbers of people; the new industries, faced with their own particular problems, have in fact contributed to the overall problem of the region (North Tyneside CDP 1978).

The case of shipbuilding illustrates the key features of decline. In 1890 UK shipbuilding amounted to 80 per cent of the world total; up to half of these vessels came from the North-East – the area built one-third of the world's ships. By the end of the 1930s the Tyneside shipbuilding industry supplied only 12 per cent of all world tonnage. Despite the long post-war boom the decline continued, with Japan now joining European competitors, and all suppliers affected by decline in demand and world over-capacity in production. In the UK this was reflected in the series of mergers, closures, nationalization and, later, privatization of the yards announced on 25 July 1984. This announcement was made shortly after the completion of the interviewing, but awareness of the proposal featured in several of the responses. The coal-mining industry presents a similar picture of contraction.

Even in times of general economic expansion the North-East has suffered. Figures for Tyne and Wear County, the major employment centre of the Northern Region providing some 40 per cent of the jobs, illustrate this. In the period from 1961 to 1976, while jobs in the country as a whole grew by about 2.3 per cent, the county's job level declined by 3 per cent. Registered unemployment rose from 5 per cent of resident labour in 1961 to 11 per cent in 1976, compared with a national rise of 3 per cent to 7 per cent. In some areas, especially the older urban areas with a traditional industrial base, the employment problem worsened.

In the recession of the 1980s, regional figures for the UK showed that, with the exception of Northern Ireland, the Northern Region had been the most severely affected. In July 1984, at the completion of the study, unemployment for the Northern Region stood at 17.9 per cent compared with the North-West, the next highest, at 15.7 per cent. This contrasted with the lowest unemployment rate, the South-East, at 9.5 per cent. The rate for Great Britain stood at 12.4 per cent (Department of Employment 1984: Dec. No. 82), and the electoral ward of 'Eldon' (a pseudonym), where the study was conducted, had 30 per cent of its economically active men and 30 per cent of its women unemployed.

Similarly, whilst the official figures for the late 1980s showed an overall decline in the level of unemployment (but in the 1990s beginning to rise once more), and although policy measures which have affected the compilation of the statistics make comparison difficult and, it is argued, produce underestimations of the actual level of unemployment,[4] the regional variations continue. Thus in August 1989, whilst the unemployment rate for the UK stood at 6.1 per cent, within this average that of the Northern Region stood at 9.2 per cent and the South-East at 3.8 per cent (Unemployment Unit and Youthaid 1989: 6). Areas within the Northern Region illuminate these differences and continuities even more markedly. Thus between 1984 and 1989, the average unemployment rate for Newcastle fell from 18.4 per cent to 12.1 per cent, whilst in 'Eldon', between April 1986 and April 1990, the total unemployment rate moved from 29.6 per cent (male – 37.8 per cent, female – 16.4 per cent) to 20 per cent (male – 28.4 per cent, female – 8.5 per cent) (Tyne and Wear County-Wide Research and Intelligence Unit 1986, 1990).

Regional restructuring has been accompanied by the general restructuring of work organization, not confined to the North-East. Thus while changes in the demand for labour not only curtail openings to a skilled trade in heavy industry, the overall reduction in such jobs and associated occupations has limited another pattern of working life: the opportunities for the construction of an uninterrupted work career formerly achieved through a succession of contracts or short-term jobs. Employment has become further casualized as employers, aided by a power shift from trade unions to employers in such times (National Economic Development Council n.d.), have sought ways of managing the recession, resulting in a reduction of core workers in well-paid, secure jobs and a growth of a secondary labour market of peripheral workers who can be set on or laid off as the economies of the firm dictate.[5] Subcontracting by large firms, contract work and short-term fixed contracts have increased. Part-time employment has grown as has sub-employment – that is, employment comprising insufficient hours or of insufficient duration to fall within the scope of protective legislation or for employees to qualify for entitlement to certain benefits. Between 1979 and 1986, part-time work in Britain rose from approximately 16 per cent to 22 per cent of the employed work force (*The Economist* 1988). 'Hidden' employment has also developed: work which is unofficially available but at rates of pay which require a subsidy from other sources, either another wage or state benefit, in order to make such work acceptable (Carr 1984; Cooke 1986; Morris 1986). The National Economic Development Council (n.d.) additionally note the flexibility achieved by changes in the patterns of overtime and shift work, the breakdown of demarcation barriers and the introduction of new pay structures.

High rates of unemployment and the changing organization of work have particularly affected the young, not only school-leavers but 'right up to the age of 25' (Lewis 1985: 2). Compared with other age groups, young people as a whole have been the most affected by unemployment. In July 1984, the year when the interviewing for the Newcastle study was completed, the unemployment rate amongst under-25s was double that of the over-25s (Lewis 1985: 2); approximately 1.2 million – that is, one in three – of the 3.1 million claimants were in this group (Department of Employment 1984: Sept.). However, whilst unemployment fell amongst school-leavers – many not entering the official statistics due to changes in accounting which excluded those on Youth Training Schemes and school-leavers (ineligible to claim benefit until September, and now ineligible even then) – the rate remained high amongst older young people. In July 1984, 25 per cent of 18- to 19-year-olds and 21 per cent of 20- to 24-year-olds were unemployed (Table 1.1).

Table 1.1 Unemployment in the United Kingdom by rates and age, July 1984

Unemployed	Under 18	18–19	20–24	25–34	35–44	45–54	55–59	60+	All ages
Males (thousands)	94.7	205.4	435.4	494.1	339.5	292.8	205.6	82.6	2,150.1
%	21.3	28.2	23.6	14.6	12.3	11.7	16.1	8.1	15.4
Females (thousands)	69.4	145.5	252.9	215.5	100.2	104.2	61.7	0.9	950.4
%	17.3	21.6	17.4	10.4	4.8	5.1	7.1	0.2	9.4
Total (thousands)	164.1	350.9	688.3	709.6	439.8	397.0	267.3	83.5	3,100.5
%	19.4	25.1	20.9	13.0	9.1	8.8	12.5	5.5	12.9

Source: Department of Employment *Employment Gazette* (September 1984, Tables 2.7 and 2.15).

Notes: While the figures are presented to one decimal place, they should not be regarded as implying precision to that degree. The figures for those aged under 20 are subject to the widest variation.

From April 1983 figures reflect the effects of the provision in the budget that some men aged 60 and over no longer sign at an employment office.

Excluded are school-leavers who could not claim benefit until September (166,653) and those on the Youth Training Scheme (283,151).

After October 1982 the system of counting the unemployed changed from registration to claimants.

Table 1.2 Unemployment in Great Britain by age, July 1979 and July 1984

Age	Number Unemployed		% Change
	1979	1984	
Under 18	258,700[c]	158,966[a]	
18–19	131,200	336,173	+156
20–24	225,500	658,901	+192
25 and over	776,700	1,824,853[b]	+135
Total	1,392,100	2,978,893	+135

Source: Department of Employment Employment Gazette (May 1980 and September 1984, cited in Lewis 1985: 3).

Notes: [a] Excludes 163,000 school-leavers and 283,151 on the Youth Training Scheme.
[b] Excludes some men over 60.
[c] Excludes 68,500 on the Youth Opportunities Programme.

(Again inspection shows a higher incidence in the North-East; in April 1986, 33.4 per cent of 18- to 24-year-olds in Newcastle were unemployed, 40.7 per cent men and 24.6 per cent women (Tyne and Wear County-Wide Research and Intelligence Unit 1986)). These figures do not include the considerable numbers of young people 'employed' under the Community Programme or on other government schemes and special measures.[6]

By July 1990, whilst still proportionately higher than for other groups, the rates had fallen to 13 per cent of 18- to 19-year-olds and 12.3 per cent of 20- to 24-year-olds unemployed. Although a substantial reduction from the previous high levels, these rates were still higher than for other age groups; they showed that more than half a million young adults (520,000) were unemployed, constituting 29.4 per cent of the unemployed population. (This excludes 16- to 17-year-olds, the majority of whom are no longer entitled to benefits) (Department of Employment 1990: July). Thus although at a lower level than during the period of the study, unemployment amongst young adults is still extensive, especially in an economy that has been expanding for eight years and when, as noted earlier, account is taken of the fact that the fall in the rate of unemployment shown in the official figures is not entirely due to an increase in the number of jobs.

Despite the implications of such data, there have been very few studies of young people[7] between the ages of 18 and 24[8]; Ashton and Maguire (n.d.: 1), at the beginning of their labour market study, point out that 'relatively little is known about the behaviour of [this age group], the young adults'. Yet, in contrast with today, a comparison of figures over the five years from July 1979 to July 1984 shows that, as well as its high incidence, the unemployment rates for the young adult had increased proportionately more than for other groups (Table 1.2). Changes in the way in which figures are collected make such comparisons difficult, especially for the under-18-year-old age group, producing underestimates in the increase in unemployment. Nonetheless, whilst recorded unemployment among over-25s more than doubled (an increase of 135 per cent), and among 18- to 19-year-olds went up two-and-a-half times (an increase of 156 per cent), among 20- to 24-year-olds it nearly trebled (an increase of 192 per cent) (Lewis 1985: 3).

A further factor of importance to young people and their families is the duration of unemployment. In July 1984, of the more than one million jobless in Great Britain who had had no work for over a year (the official definition of long-term unemployed), 30 per cent, three in every ten, were under the age of 25 (Table 1.3). Of this a total of 55,810 had not had a job for over three years (Department of Employment 1984: Sept.). Lewis noted with concern the growing number of registered unemployed who had never worked (Lewis 1985): in July 1984 over half a million people (506,842) had never

Table 1.3 Unemployment in Great Britain by age and duration of 52 weeks or longer, July 1984

Long-term unemployed	Age				
	Under 18	18	19	20–24	Total all ages
Males	6,899	25,727	34,536	159,298	907,602
as % of long-term unemployed	0.8	2.8	3.8	17.6	100
Females	4,825	17,478	21,671	83,695	268,639
as % of long-term unemployed	1.8	6.5	8.1	31.0	100
Total	11,724	43,205	56,207	242,993	1,176,241
as % of long-term unemployed	1.0	3.7	4.8	20.7	100

Source: Department of Employment *Employment Gazette* (September 1984, Table 2.6) (percentage figures are rounded up).

had a job since leaving school. Most of these were 16- and 17-year-olds but, Lewis comments, an 'alarming 179,675 of them were aged 19 or more. Five years (earlier) in July 1979 only 58,826 over 18s were in this position' (Lewis 1985: 4).

Again, towards the end of the 1980s these recorded figures showed a decline. Although there are now signs that the three-year improvement in jobless totals is drawing to an end, by July 1990 the total jobless who had been out of work for over one year had fallen by 59 per cent, to 488,182; 16 per cent (76,319) of these were between the ages of 18 and 24. Almost a fifth (14,364) had not had a job for three years or more (Department of Employment 1990: June). However, this more optimistic situation must be viewed against not only the probable under-recording of the actual numbers without jobs and the gloomy predictions about the economy but also against the kinds of jobs that young people have entered. As Elliott (1989) comments:

> All age groups, but young people in particular, have benefitted from the improvement in the figures. Amongst 18 to 24 year olds, the number unemployed for a year or more has been cut by a third over the past two months and by two thirds over the past two years. However, many of the jobs created over the past three years have been in such areas as retailing and catering which are heavily dependent on consumer spending.

The character of the youth labour market, therefore, must also be taken into account.

Labour market restructuring has particularly affected the young. Part-time and temporary work has increased proportionately more amongst young people than amongst older workers. Young people, according to Youthaid, are the 'main shock troops of the new flexible labour markets' (Youthaid 1986b: 1). Figures taken from the Government's Annual New Earnings Survey reveal that between 1979 and 1985 the proportion of teenagers in part-time jobs rose from 6 per cent to 25 per cent. For males this was a rise from 4 per cent to 19 per cent, for females 8 per cent to 30 per cent. Whilst the number of teenagers in part-time work grew from 116,000 to 407,000 – an increase of 251 per cent – that for 20- to 24-year-olds was 73 per cent, or 94,000, and for the over-25s a similar number, 97,000, but representing under 3 per cent of the part-time workers in this age group (Lewis 1987). This growth in part-time work has, moreover, been matched by the growth in short-term jobs, especially for the under-18s. Part-time work is likely to be temporary work. In 1985 the under-18s in work had a more than one in five chance of becoming unemployed within any three months, but those out of work had a three in four chance of getting a job in the same period. The older the group, the less each of these probabilities. For the 20- to 24-year-old age group, the chances are respectively one in eleven and one in two; for the 45- to 54-year-old age group they are one in fifty and one in four. Older people, therefore, are more secure in their jobs, but once unemployed they have less chance of obtaining full-time work. For young people the 'pattern of employment is change and insecurity, a process of moving in and out of work' (Youthaid 1986b: 1).

This new flexible labour market is further promoted by the deregulation of the pay and working conditions of young people. The 1986 Wages Act, for example, removes workers under the age of 21 from the protection of the Wages Councils, bodies which have traditionally set the minimum standards for low-paid, poorly unionized industries such as hotel and catering, hairdressing and retailing, industries in which young people form one-third of the work-force. The Act weakens the rights covering unfair deductions from pay; and under the 1985 Board and Lodging Regulations, young workers (but not older workers) in tied accommodation also lose protection against high board and lodging charges. (One-fifth of hotel workers are under 21.) It is feared that the Wages Act heralds a spiral of undercutting by encouraging employers to use young people as a cheap source of labour, dismissing them in favour of their younger peers when they become entitled to the full adult rate (Byrne 1986). More recent legislation allows night work and has removed young people from the legal protection of limits on the number of hours which can be worked.

These issues have been compounded by the age structure of the population; the number of young people entering the labour market has been greater than the numbers retiring. In 1982 it was estimated that an extra 150,000 jobs a year were needed just to stop unemployment rising (Metcalf 1982). Although by the mid-1990s demographic changes will have affected this balance, producing a shortage of young workers, the economy threatens to enter a further recession and regional imbalances in employment prospects continue. The fear remains, therefore, that not only might the young generation of the early 1980s, some of whom were interviewed for this study, continue to suffer from poor employment prospects, but that new cohorts will share their experience.

FAMILY RELATIONSHIPS AND SOCIAL CHANGE

The interviews with families who took part in the pilot study revealed how central to individual and family lives were the changes attendant upon this poor and unpredictable labour market and how complex the possible ramifications. The realization led to a re-ordered research design which made change and flux pivotal to the investigation, replacing the original comparison between the families of employed and unemployed young people. For the changes taking place affected all families, not just those of the unemployed. The theoretical and methodological importance of this re-orientation is described in Appendix Two.

The chapters that follow take up the theme of change and uncertainty in different ways. Not all the areas of young people's lives are covered, and only some of the issues can be pursued in the space of a book. What the responses of young people and their parents to the vagaries of the labour market show is how such changes penetrate the layers of social existence and colour the minutiae of individual and family lives. The effects of unemployment and job insecurity, as several studies have noted, do not halt at the individual, nor are they purely economic.

Chapter Two focuses on the labour market. It looks at the impact of change on family members in three ways. It would be impossible to identify all the movements in and out of paid employment that were experienced by the people in the study. However, by noting changes in employment status at particular points in the histories of all family members, it is possible to capture a sense of the flux which a restructuring labour market brings to family life. The kaleidoscopic nature of the changing employment statuses is captured through summary snapshot representations. The chapter also looks at how families deploy their resources in the effort to help young people obtain paid employment and the effect of a changing labour market upon these resources themselves, highlighting the interdependence of public and private resources. It then turns to young people's experience of the labour market within the context of the shifts in the power relationship between employer and employee.

Chapter Two provides the context for the rest of the book. Against the background of labour market experience and family involvement, Chapter Three looks at how the labour market affects a young person's transition to independence within the family. It looks at the historical roots of independence in family life and their connection with elements of the work ethic, showing how the notion of work, the value of money, reliability and self-sufficiency are embedded in family routines and practices. It shows how paid employment affects family statuses and relationships through the economic, social and cultural power conferred, and the effect of the labour market on the progression to adulthood and full citizenship.

Chapter Four traces some of the ways a poor labour market can dislodge individuals not only from a sense of personal order and direction but also from the general social order. It shows how routines and schedules are disrupted in ways that undermine a sense of belonging, create social divisions and produce disjunctions and contradictions for other family members as well as the unemployed member. This is reflected in the language and metaphor of sickness and well-being through which people express their experiences.

Chapter Five focuses on values and the moral community, taking up the themes of social contract, fairness, reciprocity and trust. It shows how job shortages and chronic anxiety about obtaining and retaining paid employment bring to the fore contradictions in values. It looks at how such values are mediated through the choices family members make and in the values they try to sustain, and how in turn these decisions contribute to the ambience of the wider society.

The book is about ordinary families; they were not selected because they had problems. All lived in a working-class neighbourhood of Newcastle upon Tyne; all parents were skilled, semiskilled or unskilled workers; but within this the families displayed a heterogeneity of circumstances, ranging from comparative affluence (ownership of home, caravan and boat in one case) to extreme poverty, some dependent entirely on state benefit. Thus even in an area with the high rate of unemployment noted earlier in this chapter, families could inhabit different worlds whilst living within a few yards of each other, just as some individuals did within the same family. Nonetheless, all were affected by economic change, and the book attempts to give voice to the uncertainties such change produced, tracing the effects into some of the corners of individual and family lives. There is no attempt to generalize the findings of the study in any statistical sense; in a study confined to forty families, regionally and socially located, this is not possible. What the study does, however, is identify some of the familial processes through which public and private domains penetrate each other and some of the costs of a restructuring economy.

2

LOCAL LABOUR MARKETS AND THE HOUSEHOLD

Change and flux

INTRODUCTION

Industrial restructuring, a contracting labour market and changing patterns of work meant that the Newcastle families were caught up in an unpredictable and changing situation. Family members were not only subject to shifts in their employment statuses – moving between employment, unemployment, sub-employment and part-time jobs – but they also had to cope with changing labour market norms. In responding to these changes they also found that the resources upon which they could draw were losing their currency.

Studies of the flow between employment and unemployment show that the unemployed are not a static group (Daniel 1981). Although some unemployed people never obtain work, or remain unemployed for long periods, the majority, especially the young (Central Statistical Office, 1984), do gain employment – some in permanent jobs, others to become unemployed once more – whilst those in apparently secure jobs can lose them.

The concept of unemployment flow has been used to describe aggregates; however, by thinking of the flow in and out of employment in terms of individuals' employment careers,[1] the notion chimes well with individual experience in a volatile labour market. From the perspective of the family this takes on added significance, for the family is where the employment careers of individuals as family members coincide, intersecting with each other in a setting which is patterned by its own particular norms and structures of statuses and roles. Thus not only might a family member experience change in his or her own employment career, but he or she could also be living within the ambience of change in others' lives and be part of any ensuing shift in the pattern of relationships between family members as they move in and out of employment. The effect of a poor and deteriorating local labour market upon familial age and gender relationships, and the significance, for example, for power, authority, dependence, independence and equity, is taken up in later chapters.

A striking feature of the study was the extent to which a changing labour market penetrated family life. This chapter looks at three aspects of this intersection between family and the labour market. The first aspect is how the configuration of employment statuses within a family could change as family members gained and lost jobs; some families seemed to be living in a constant state of flux, producing a climate of uncertainty. The second aspect shows how, in the attempts of young family members to gain and retain a place within the labour market, resources are drawn upon, and how they also are affected by the changing labour market. The third section looks at the flux and uncertainty in the labour market experience of young adults and the changing, or perhaps only more explicit, norms which govern the relationships between employer and employee and which were caused by the changing labour market.

FAMILY CONFIGURATIONS
OF EMPLOYMENT

The poor labour market brought such complexity into the lives of the Newcastle families that it is important to capture and make visible some of the elements which contributed to it.

In an area such as Eldon where unemployment rates had been high and rising, many households were likely to experience change in the employment statuses of their members. This is especially true of those households which contain young people, a group whose vulnerability to unemployment is statistically greater than other age groups and which tends to include relatively higher numbers of people of working age. Thus, as noted, many households were coping with or fearing the unemployment of not only one member.

Retrospective data for the period from January 1980 up to the start of the study in 1983 shows, for example, that in most of the Eldon households one or more members had been unemployed, made redundant, been sub-employed or employed intermittently, or were on a work training or work experience scheme sponsored by the Manpower Services Commission (MSC). Almost half of the young people had parents who had been touched by unemployment over the past five years. To make matters more complicated, most of the households contained more than one young person aged over 16; thus most of the informants had siblings who were in or trying to enter the labour force.

Moreover, although the study focused primarily on the two-generation household of parents and children still living in the parental home, additional complexity arose from the fact that a family's intimate experience of the labour market stemmed in part from the employment careers of those siblings now living outside the household. This was not only because the early years in the labour market had been spent in the parental home, but also because since setting up their own homes these children often had continuing and frequent contact with parents. Many adult children were regular visitors to their parents' household and, in some cases, were part of the daily life, sharing experiences and offering help, advice and criticism.

Changes in employment statuses within the Newcastle families were at times extensive. To take one example, in the five years preceding the interviewing in late 1983 and early 1984, the Hills family had seen the following changes:

1 Mr Hills moved onto night shift when the shipyard where he worked a day shift closed down.
2 Mrs Hills changed from one part-time job to another because of redundancy (and she had been told she was to be made redundant again in the near future).
3 Frank Hills left school in 1978 at age 18, was unemployed for two months, took a temporary job and in 1979 secured a steady job in the Civil Service.
4 Keith Hills left school in 1979, completed a university degree in 1982 and was unemployed from mid-1982 onwards.
5 Margaret Hills left school in 1981, was unemployed until mid-1983, and then worked part-time until November of that year, when she was offered full-time employment.

Fluctuations of this kind are captured for the group as a whole, albeit in a limited way, by comparing the configurations of family employment statuses at different times (Table 2.1). The kaleidoscopic nature of the changes is suggested by the differences between the

Table 2.1 Family employment status configurations at three time periods

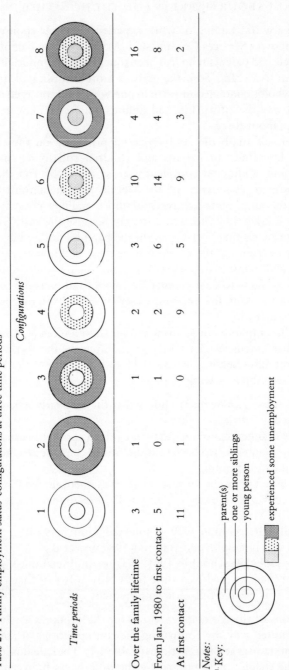

Time periods	Configurations[1]							
	1	2	3	4	5	6	7	8
Over the family lifetime	3	1	1	2	3	10	4	16
From Jan. 1980 to first contact	5	0	1	2	6	14	4	8
At first contact	11	1	0	9	5	9	3	2

Notes:
[1] Key:

- parent(s)
- one or more siblings
- young person

  experienced some unemployment

To represent change in an accessible way, a family configuration is condensed to three components: the young person, siblings as a group—including those no longer living in the parental home—and fathers or single parent. The extent of unemployment and the fluctuations in status are under-represented because of the exclusion of the mother in two-parent households, the compression of sibling unemployment into one indicator (any unemployment amongst siblings) and the fact that the time periods are summaries of experience. These temporal comparisons do not show transformations within individual families.

'snapshot' picture at first contact and the limited longitudinal data taken from 1980 up to the time of this contact in 1983–4. For example, the number of families apparently unaffected by unemployment shrinks from eleven at the contact stage to five for the earlier period; and when the lifetime of the family is taken into account, only three families remain untouched by unemployment.

Similar changes are reflected in all the figures. Thus amongst the young people themselves, at the time of the first contact they fell almost equally between employed (twenty-two) and unemployed (eighteen). However, when their earlier experiences in the labour market were taken into account, only seven young people had been in full-time, continuous employment since leaving school. Moreover, when family history is included, only three came from families with no record of unemployment; the others were from families with a mixture of unemployment amongst siblings and parents. Unemployment had touched both generations in twenty-one families; in fifteen only the younger generation had experienced it, sometimes the young person alone, sometimes one or more siblings, sometimes both. Intermittent employment is not recorded here between January 1980 and the time of first contact, but even this limited presentation shows that change had taken place in twenty-four families.

However, it was not only the number of family members affected and the frequency of the changes in employment status that penetrated family life; it was also the unpredictability of the changes. Such changes occurred during the period of contact with the families, and the methodological problems to which this gave rise are noted in Appendix Two.

For the families, such events could bring elation or searing uncertainty to family life. Kathleen McGuinness found employment in the few weeks between the screening survey and a telephone call made to arrange an interview with her, as her delighted mother explained. In the Fox family, however, where there had been little unemployment until recently, there was now a sudden reversal of circumstances. Mr Fox, whose experience of unemployment had been limited to a few days in 1958 and a few weeks in 1971 following fifteen-and-a-half years in the Army, was unexpectedly made redundant from his job of twelve years' standing. Ironically, in an interview before receiving this news, his wife had emphasized the family's relatively fortunate position, remarking, 'I feel really sorry for those who aren't in the position we are in.' It contrasted with

27

the situation a few weeks later as Mr Fox looked into the future, revealing the changes which recession can bring to a household:

> At the moment I would say for the next 12 months I'm fairly comfortable, obviously having to rely on my redundancy pay, but what it's gonna be like in 12 months' time, it's very difficult to say. I might be fortunate enough to, in a month's time, . . . have another full-time job with a *good* income, but if over the next 12 months I'm not lucky enough to get another job. Jenny [his younger child] is going to be coming out of the 12 months scheme [Youth Training Scheme (YTS), which had replaced the Youth Opportunities Programme (YOP)] shortly. I'm hoping Paul is going to be fortunate enough to get a *full*-time job out of what he's doing at the moment [16 hours per week] and if there's nothing happens with the school ladies – because there's talk . . . at the moment, that they were going to make cut-backs on the school meals and the supervisors and things like that. But if it boils down to myself being on the dole, Jenny *and* my wife, and just Paul working, I think that . . . after a 12-month period, yes, I think we're going to find things difficult then (emphasis in original).

That security could so suddenly and unpredictably be swept away sounds a note of caution if those few families who had escaped unemployment are to be considered a special group against which to compare others. These families, like the rest, were aware they were living in a changing economic environment. Husbands cites opinion poll evidence showing that in May 1983 'a third of the electorate were personally affected by unemployment or in a family where another member was so affected' (Husbands 1985: 14). He suggests that the percentage of the population also with neighbours or local acquaintances who were unemployed or perceived as likely to be unemployed must amount to solid majorities of the electorate. Indeed, in the three core families in the Newcastle study – those with no experience of unemployment – anxieties about obtaining and retaining jobs were expressed. There was, for example, a sense that their relatively secure circumstances were due to sheer good fortune, as Martin Pearce observed: 'I think even when I was at school they [parents] were worried about us not getting a job. I think they, myself, were surprised how lucky I was. I still say that I was really lucky.' And concealed within his official record of continuous employment is a period of anxiety between his receiving four months' notice from the firm in which he was then working and his finding his present job, which he did before his notice was worked out.

In another case, Mark Freeman's father commented, 'Things seemed to work out exactly as we expected. There was no sort of hassle or hold up. We were just lucky, that's all.' Yet when asked about the experiences of her friends and kin, Mrs Freeman – in this household in which both parents and both children were employed and in which no one had ever been entered on the official unemployment register – revealed the context of anxiety in which their own apparent good fortune and her son's apprenticeship was understood:

> One friend in particular, . . . [her son] didn't get a job, but I have relatives, some of them are on schemes and things like that, y'know. Not many apprenticeships in that age group. Most of Mark's friends couldn't get jobs, y'know. He was sort of one of the elite.

Later in the interview, reflecting on her experience as a parent, she drew attention to the strains of parenthood during a recession, even for those who seem to be secure:

> I think if you knew . . . what was in store for you, I don't know whether I would do it again. I enjoyed them when they were little, but since they've grown up I've found it harder to cope – not because of them, because of me. I tend to worry, I worry about their future and things like that. . . .When Mark was coming up to leaving school and you knew that things were bad, I used to say, 'If only he gets a job I'll be the happiest woman on earth'. Fortunately he did, but then there's no guarantee that he's going to keep the job.

Only one family, the Hewitts, seemed confident. But even here there was concern over the possibility of a daughter considering marriage to someone without a job. It was deemed highly unlikely to happen because the girl was 'too sensible'. Yet the unpredictability of the labour market could prove them wrong.

As the study proceeded it became clear that this group of core families not only shared the stress and uncertainties arising from a poor labour market, but it also was indistinguishable from most of the others in terms of the pressures, encouragements and family routines which underpinned what were considered to be proper attitudes towards work and job seeking, and in the way the changing labour market affected their resources. The important part played in the study by this group, therefore, was to highlight the way the changing labour market intruded upon all the families.

RESOURCES AND THE SEARCH FOR JOBS

At all times entry into the labour market and progression through employment careers are shaped by the resources upon which people can draw. Although the boundaries are blurred, resources may belong to the individual – in, for example, such attributes as educational qualifications and reputation – or they may stem from others – for example, in an individual's access to information or in privileged entry through the contacts of kin and friends. When valued assets such as proper jobs are scarce (themselves a key resource) people turn even more eagerly to the resources they can muster in their effort to secure or retain a foothold in the labour market.

Resources, of course, vary amongst families and amongst family members. They are influenced by position in the class and occupational structure and by the distribution of wealth as well as by age and gender. Limits, however, are not only imposed by the extent of a family's stock of such goods; in times of technological and social change resources themselves become vulnerable. They can lose their currency or be swept away altogether. Thus change in the value of resources themselves was part of the changing environment in which young people and their families were living, contributing a further dimension to the flux and uncertainty.

To speak of a family's resources conceals the fact that although some resources may be held more or less collectively, others belong to individual members. Resources, moreover – regardless of who owns them – cannot be used or transferred without incurring change: realignments and obligations among family members through the media of gifts, loans, services, compassion and so forth. The conceptualization of resources in the economist's terminology, discussed in the opening chapter, draws attention not only to the range, availability and ownership of resources but also to the forms of exchange and the processes which are set in motion within a family by a restructuring labour market. These issues are deferred to later chapters. The concern here is with resources as such and their currency in young people's search for jobs.

Young people's resources

At the point of entry into the labour market there are some resources which young people hold as of right. These include cultural capital, which derives from educational qualifications and access to the services provided by the state through the careers service and job centres. Such cultural capital is, of course, connected to other types of resources. Qualifications, for example, are the outcome not only of individual effort, intelligence and institutional provision but are also shaped by the social and cultural capital of parental knowledge, advice, encouragement and the social networks which enhance educational opportunities. Similarly, parental economic capital can be critical to young people's accumulation of resources, such economic provision ranging from substantial school fees to the minor expense of bus fare to subsidize visits to the careers office. The distinction made between the formal and informal means of obtaining employment, frequently used in the job search literature, conceals these critical connections between the private and public domains.

Most of the young people in the study had taken some public examinations, largely CSE. A minority had one or more O levels or their CSE equivalent.[2] Martin Pearce had five, but no one else had more than three. Both parents and young people were asked how relevant they felt educational qualifications were in a young person's search for work.

The responses reveal a shifting and uncertain scene. With a few exceptions parents and young people expressed negative views about the role played by educational qualifications in helping young people to get jobs. It was not that all had formerly held qualifications in high esteem or even thought them necessary, but that the ground rules seemed to be shifting. The demand for qualifications seemed arbitrary. The metaphor of the racecourse, where set and recognizable hurdles had to be cleared in order to reach a predetermined finishing post, was replaced by that of a circus ring, where arbitrary hoops were leapt through to the demands of idiosyncratic ringmasters. Some parents and young people felt that qualifications such as GCE and CSE were entirely, or largely, irrelevant as far as jobs were concerned. They appeared neither to have bearing upon the type of job ultimately obtained nor to be any protection against unemployment. Most informants were able to cite qualified individuals, known to them personally or to their friends, who were nonetheless unemployed or in unskilled occupations. As Mr Ryan said, 'I don't think qualifications has got anything to do with [getting jobs], 'cos I know boys that's got O levels and A levels and they're labouring on the roadways.'

Such awareness could reverberate upon decisions about extended schooling, a worrying effect for a region where the taking up of education beyond compulsory school-leaving age is low. Mrs Rice argued, 'I know children who have sat for O levels and A levels and they cannot get a job, you know. I just honestly didn't think it was worth [my sons] staying on.' There was also doubt that spending time improving one's level of qualification while unemployed would pay off, as Philip Thompson reasoned:

> You see people, even graduates nowadays, they haven't got jobs . . . and people with O levels who haven't got jobs, nine in ten. So there's me, with sort of like CSEs gonna go to college for a year and trying to get O levels . . . and I'd still be on the scrap heap, wouldn't I? So it seems a waste of a year.

Moreover, employers' demands for qualifications seemed irrational and arbitrary. Thus Mrs Jones commented, 'Even the shop jobs for counter assistants, they're making the standards that high it's just too ridiculous for words.' Carol Knight, unemployed for almost a year when interviewed, felt the demands for qualifications were being steadily increased, rendering her own CSE passes useless: 'When I first left school it was, they all wanted CSEs and the next year it was all O levels and now this year it's A levels.'

Raising demands was no doubt a way of dealing with an over-abundance of applications. It nonetheless devalued and rendered worthless formerly acceptable currency. Yet in other cases qualifications had not even been asked for or needed. Kathleen McGuiness, when asked if her exam results had helped her to get a job, said:

Well, up until now, no, because it was always that I knew someone. At the supermarket he said it was my handwriting, so I don't know if my exams had anything to do with that. . . . Up until now nobody's said, 'Oh, I like your exam results'.

Even those who had always been employed and found work of the kind they liked and wanted were becoming unconvinced of the value of qualifications. Martin Pearce, referred to earlier, a trainee auditing clerk with five O levels, believed he had secured his current post through having 'experience' as opposed to being the best qualified applicant. He also noted the tension between qualifications and the social capital of family contacts which a poor labour market seemed to be revealing: 'At one time I think it used to be exams but you've got people with degrees and all sorts on the dole [and] there's people with nothing who've got into a good job because their family's in it.'

There were, however, some parents who recognized the increased importance of qualifications. Mrs Bryant, for example, explained how she had tried in vain to persuade her younger daughter to go to college for a year at sixteen.

She got a list of jobs and on every job it says, 'Prefer those with one year's college.' And I said, 'Look at that. . . . There's eight jobs there and there's only *one* [for] which you haven't got to go to college.' 'I don't want to go, I don't want to go.' I says, 'Fair enough, . . . but don't come crying to me if you cannot get a job. You'll find out in years to come that you need qualifications to get a job.'

Mr Phillips hoped his younger able son would 'stick out' for his O levels and then get his A levels and to 'never mind the lads' calling him, 'swot'. '"Forget about them, he'll be sweeping the streets," I says. "You can be up in a bloody good job later on in life."'

Yet amongst those who had conformed to the requirements of the educational system, there were now doubts about the legitimacy of its claims. They felt they had been misled. Hugh Clark, with one O level and eight CSE passes at Grades 2 and 3, had been unemployed for almost a year and was studying one day a week at college for a City and Guilds qualification in computing. He had previously been on several schemes, including a year on a training course at an ITEC (Information Technology Centre). But, as his father observed:

He's on this City and Guilds and after that, that's it. What can he do after that? . . . He's tried everywhere and done everything what they told him to do. He went to school from when he was 5 till he was 16. They says his exams was important and so he sat all the exams, never had a day off school. On the day he left school, he got his reference, he got all his exam results, passed them, and then still no job.

Similar comments about their conformity to a system that had failed them were made by the mother of a graduate son. A study by Ashton and Maguire (n.d.) of the young adult labour market in four regions sheds some light on the paradox by revealing the primacy of the local labour market over qualifications and other personal attributes. In Sunderland, an area with similarly high levels of unemployment, the less qualified were more likely to obtain work than were those qualified with A levels and over.[3]

There was a loss of credibility in other state agencies to which young people turned in their search for employment; for the same poor labour market meant that few could be directed into jobs by either the careers service or, for those over eighteen years of age, the job centre. The devaluation of these resources raised dilemmas for the users and contradictions in the services.

Some recognized that the fault did not lie with the services themselves. 'They do the best they could do to find you a job', and 'are quite good really [considering] there are so many on the dole. Every time I go along they gave us the best advice they could,' were the comments of two unemployed young people, Christine Dyer and Umar Kahn. The views of many parents on the difficulties and responses of the careers service were summed up by Mr Hamilton, who had eventually helped his son to get a labouring job at his own place of work:

I think basically they just fob them off . . . stick them in a YOP scheme or what have you. . . .There's not really a great deal they can do. . . .They have to operate in a climate of unemployment, so it makes it very difficult for them to really operate effectively, possibly the way they *want* to work.

A feeling that the job centres had little to offer was similarly widespread. Geoffrey Lewis complained, 'Them divent really offer you much,' and Mrs Clark felt that the service was 'very poor. . . .There's nothing there . . . there's just no jobs. . . .I mean, it's like beating your head against a brick wall.'

Thus of the thirty-one who, on leaving school, approached the careers service (Table 2.2), only four were directly placed in jobs, and only one person found a job through the job centre, although most of those who had been unemployed made visits. The rest of the school-leavers, twenty-seven, had been placed on YOP training schemes,[4] but only seven had been kept on. By the time of the interviews only two, a carpet-fitter and a word-processor operator, were still working with their YTS employers. No doubt this kind of experience coloured evaluations of the usefulness of the service.

Credibility was further undermined by the effect of the fierce competition for jobs and the pressures this placed on the careers service and job centre personnel young people met. For example, a job could be taken before an applicant even arrived, although directed there by the careers officer, as Michael West complained:

Table 2.2 Placements of young people through the careers service

Placed in a job (total: 4)	Placed on YOP(s) (leading to a job) (total: 7)	Placed on YOP(s) not leading to a job (total: 20)
Shirley Hewitt	Karen Hughes	Kathy Page
Marie Davis	Bryan Jones	Dawn Harris
Phil Matthews	Caroline Price	Sandra Cross
Martin Pearce	Hilary Jenkins	Christine Dyer
	John Phillips	Angela Ward
	Martin Johnson	Carol Knight
	Malcolm Bryant	Kathleen McGuinness
		Joanna McGuire
		Cheryl Reynolds
		Kevin Ryan
		Ian Potter
		Michael West
		Philip Thompson
		Peter Hamilton
		Neil Peters
		Paul Fox
		Geoffrey Lewis
		Stuart Drake
		Umar Kahn
		Hugh Clark

> They had sent us for a job once and when I got in there the job had already been took. . . .Them were just muckin' yer about . . . and they wanna keep an eye on their files, an' all, 'cos they lost mine. I was sitting there for two hours while they looked for it.

Because of the young people's limited economic resources, such experiences raised dilemmas for them. Visits to the offices cost money and when persistent visiting did not result in a job, the question arose as to whether the economic outlay was worth making. Thus one unemployed young man, although still hoping to find a job, had resigned himself to continuing unemployment:

> Oh, I used to gan there nearly all the time. But after a while I was just getting sick, yer know, paying all me dole money out in bus fares to get up the town, get there, they'd say, 'Oh, why, there's only government schemes.' Waste of time, complete waste of time. After a while I thought to myself, 'Why, look at all the money you've spent.' I've got nowhere so I might as well give in, yer know, save me money.

> (Stuart Drake)

Indeed, in some cases travel costs were deemed prohibitive. Several said that the cost of bus fares to the careers centre in the city had deterred them from making more frequent visits. Karen Hughes said she would 'definitely' have gone more often had it not been for the cost (26 pence each way). Kevin Ryan, who had fares of 32 pence each way to pay, said, 'I would have went more often, but . . . me mam couldn't afford it.' His comment indicates the importance of a family's economic resources for those on the fringes of the labour market, an issue which is taken up later.

There was a further paradox. Persistence in the search for work – generally deemed an admirable and essential quality – could evoke a demoralizing response from the staff of a hard-pressed careers service. Many young people began their search for work by making regular and frequent visits to the careers office. Often enthusiasm waned as the months passed, but David Mitchell, now working ac a labourer, claimed he had been told not to call every day. His mother complained, 'The woman used to play war with them and say, "D'you know, this is no good trailing here every day . . . there isn't any jobs. . . .[Y]ou should stop in the house, just come about twice a week."' Paul Fox, working part-time for a security firm, recalled a similar experience: 'I was up there three times a week. . . .[O]ne of the lasses said they were sick of us'.

In other instances, young people encountered assumptions about their local geographical mobility: a job centre would only agree to arrange interviews with firms in the immediate neighbourhood of their home. This localism was overcome, especially by those with their own transport, by multi-registration. John Phillips, suddenly made redundant after two years, adopted his girlfriend's successful strategy of visiting several job centres in the region. Implicitly challenging any bureaucratic centralism. Mr Phillips, his father, explained:

> He's been to Stanley, Consett, Chester-le-Street, the whole of the job shops, looking for places. . . .He's went all over the place looking at different job shops, trying to find a job. . . .anywhere. He's got his own transport. . . .the motor − . . . not *just* . . . the local ones . . .

It is, however, a method which is only possible for those who are not reliant on public transport, who have been able to accumulate material resources of their own or who can turn to friends or relatives for help. As noted, even the cost of travel on public transport can become prohibitive for those solely reliant on supplementary benefit and who come from families who cannot afford to subsidize them. This leads to a consideration of other resources upon which young people could draw in the search for work, particularly family resources, and the effect of the recession upon them.

Family Resources

On leaving school, when unemployed young people had little money, family members, particularly parents, subsidized the search for work in a variety of ways. As well as fares to the careers office or job centre, subsidies included postage for letters of application, fees, and material goods. 'He wrote literally hundreds of letters,' said Mrs Pierce. 'It cost his father a small fortune in stamps.' Mr Bryant, well aware of his economic sacrifice, offered his daughter support amounting to bribery to take up secretarial studies:

We wanted her to go to the poly and push herself on. I says,
'I know you want to leave school and get some money for
yourself. Well, I'll give you a few quid a week. I know *I'll* be
getting nothing off you but it doesn't matter, it's getting you
on that matters.' (emphasis in original).

He recognized the importance of developing the child's own
cultural capital by way of qualifications and was drawing upon his
knowledge of the workings of the labour market, his social capital.
Others benefitted from such material resources as car ownership in
the family, coupled with a willingness to convert it for use in the
job search. As Angela Ward said:

My brother-in-law . . . often . . . drops us off at the job centre
– like if I've been a message with him, he'll say, 'Run in and
see if there's any jobs.' . . . I normally go in. . . .I mean, you
might as well go in and have a look.

Job searching took place against the background of each family's
particular ethos, an aspect of cultural capital which included attitudes
towards work and the shaping of work identities over the years. The
practices surrounding this are discussed in the next chapter. The
outcome, however, was, or had been, a general expectation that on
entering the labour market children would find paid employment.

Martin'll work because he's been brought up in a house where
you have to work. I mean Martin will sometimes say to us,
'Oh Mum, I'm not well.' I'll say, 'Have you got pneumonia,
pet?' He'll say, 'No.' I'll say, 'Well, you can go to work.' *That*
is the way *we* are (emphasis in original).

(Mrs Pierce)

Such an orientation to work in the face of scarce jobs was sustained
in many families by persistent encouragement and insistence on
continued searching.

Sometimes she used to say, 'Oh I'm not going to write any
more, it isn't worth it.' I used to say, 'Why, keep trying,
something will turn up for you.' She kept going and she got
something.

(Mrs Reynolds)

I tried to tell him – Malcolm – and Jennifer, 'Go *looking* for it.
If you sit on your backsides, it's not going to come *here* for

you. Nobody's going to knock on this door and say, "Will
you come and work for me?" You've gotta go to them, say,
"Can *I* work for *you*?"' (emphasis in original).

(Mr Bryant)

My husband said to him, 'Well mind, there's no lying in bed,
you're up and you're out *looking* whether you get one or not.
You're not getting away [with] idling in bed.' So that's exactly
what the lad done (emphasis in original).

(Mrs Mitchell)

Such pressures had, of course, an effect upon other aspects of family
relationships; this is taken up in later chapters.

Parents, both mothers and fathers, also gave their children
emotional and moral support. Although, without the appropriate
social capital, they frequently felt powerless to help in more practical
ways, they attempted to preserve the young person's 'spirit' and
to prevent despondency from developing into despair. When his
daughter was unemployed for a long period, Mr Hills said, 'I
mean, we took an interest but . . . I work in the shipyards, there
was nothing for her down at the *yards*, I used to say, you know,
"Don't lose heart", and all that.' Support, however, could also take
the opposite form – supporting a young person's decision not to
search for work when jobs or YOPs were seen as exploitative and
providing such little reward.

Such cultural and moral support drew upon time and energy
as well as emotion. There were many instances where parental
resources were converted into emotional capital for the benefit of
the child. Some parents, for example, would give their time by
accompanying a child to the careers centre or take them to the
place of interview to ensure finding it; or comb the job columns
of the newspaper, either separately or with a son or daughter. As
Mrs Hughes said:

If she was in we would go through [the paper] together, but if
I was on my own I would look in the *Journal* of a morning and
things like that. If there was any job advertised in the shops
or anything like that as her father was walking past he'd say,
'Well, I've seen this.' He'd write the telephone number down
and bring it home.

Finally, there was the social capital of knowledge, information
and connections with the labour market. The social capital which

young people might build up is referred to later in the chapter; and the impact upon the power relationships within the family of the interplay between the economic, cultural and social resources which a job gave the young adult is one of the themes of the next chapter. For parents, ownership of social capital might be converted into advice for their children, encouragement to improve skills and privileged access to jobs. Knowledge about how the labour market works enabled parents to offer advice on matters such as how to write letters of application, how to behave at an interview, what to wear and where to go to look for work. 'Malcolm was going round, on *my* advice,' said Mr Bryant. 'Round different little industrial estates . . . knocking on doors trying to find employment.' Mrs Hughes had helped Karen with her job applications: 'She always used to sit with me and I used to help her with the letters – tell her what [was] the best things to say and that.' Mrs Davis had advised her daughter to take an example of her needlework to an interview for a sewing job:

> [I said] to take something to show, just like a blouse. She thought I was stupid at first. I says, 'Don't sit back, keep asking different things about the job.' And she just took that blouse and they said it was very good.

This interview led to a job, still held three and a half years later. Mrs Jenkins had helped her daughter, Hilary, 'to fill forms in, forms for the Electricity Board and places like that. I took her once when she had to go for an interview and she didn't know where the place was.'

Sometimes parental advice was superior to that given by the careers staff; for example, a father's advice to dress 'scruffy' when interviewed for certain low-skilled work. Some parents, as noted, recognized the value of skills despite the apparently arbitrary nature of the labour market. In addition, some parents had access, through persons located in other parts of the social structure, to information and advice beyond what they knew from personal experience and observation. For example, as a part-time youth leader and through conversations with a careers officer, one father had been able to advise his daughter that she could register at several careers offices. This advice had not yet brought results, but he felt pleased that he had been able to offer a different approach. Mrs Pierce's ability to discuss her son's job as a trainee accountant with her dentist enabled her to use his general knowledge of professional life when he reassured her that low wages at the training stage were a characteristic of the profession and suggested her son would be wise to tolerate them in anticipation of the prospects the job offered.

This does not quite fall into the category of inside information[5] since the knowledge is available to all who enquire. Similarly, people in work who watched the works notice-boards for vacancies which were also publicly advertised, or who collected generally available application forms as soon as they were issued, were privileged only in the sense of having earlier access to information and thus the ability to get friends or relatives into the formal selection procedures early.

Nonetheless, the social capital of social networks did supply information on the availability of jobs, and personal recommendation in some cases helped a young person to get a job. Examining the availability and use of this resource illustrates how resources can be affected by a changing local labour market.

Social capital

There was a feeling amongst young people and their parents that getting a job was a matter of who you knew rather than what you knew. As Mrs Kelly said, 'Kids haven't got a chance unless they've got somebody to speak for them.' Friends, neighbours and above all kin were seen as people who might make a recommendation to an employer, supply information about job vacancies or, if self-employed, offer a job. As well as the tradition of 'speaking for' in some occupations, there is evidence that in a poor labour market personal recommendation is a useful screening mechanism for a hard-pressed personnel department (Jenkins *et al.* 1983). For young people in the North-East, however, the changing character of the local labour market meant that the social capital vested in the affective networks of kins and friends was both becoming scarce and losing its currency. As Philip Thompson observed, 'Me mam always asks, but everybody's in the same boat.'

The value of networks as resources was declining in several ways. In the first place, much depended upon the type of work connections kin and friends had, especially through their own employment either currently or in the past. The high rate of adult and youth unemployment in the area, the decline in the traditional industries and the changing structure of work witnessed in the increase in part-time, temporary and contract work reduced the extent to which networks were or could be embedded in the labour market. There were fewer jobs, and those with jobs were not necessarily secure in them. Moreover, people who were seen as possible work contacts might be employed in organizations with highly bureaucratized selection procedures where personal recommendation counted for little, or in inappropriate sectors of the market. For example, whilst jobs that were seen as particularly exploitative were deemed unsuitable for young people of either sex, some of the limits upon the usefulness of networks were those of gender and age. As noted earlier, Mr Hills recognized his inability to help his daughter: 'I mean . . . there was nothing for her down at the yards.' On the other hand, Mrs McGuinness discussed with her older son whether or not his teenage sister should accept a cleaning job they had heard about, the kind of job in which the mother had been formerly employed but which she felt was unsuitable for a young girl. Chaney (1985) has described the efficiency of women's social networks in transmitting information about such vacancies in a deteriorating and hence more competitive labour market. Her evidence also shows that women returning to work increasingly take up domestic/cleaning jobs. This suggests, however, that normative boundaries might be breached if young females were to draw upon such social networks for employment in this sector.

As well as the place of employment, a contact's status as an employee – both by position in the organization and by reputation – also counted. Mr Fox, a supervisor, observed about his son, 'I managed to get him a job with our firm. It wasn't solely through me that he got it, but obviously, the position I held did help it'. (Ironically Mr Fox was later made redundant).

In our society, however, there are moral (as well as organizational) limits upon this use of social capital, and several respondents emphasized that the young people they had 'spoken for' were still subject to formal selection procedures. Such constraints upon ties of affectivity were clear in the reaction of Mrs Pearce's brother who, when asked if he could find work for his nephew, asked how he could take on a nephew when he was laying off forty men the next day. The aspect of moral justice and fairness in this incident is discussed more generally in Chapter Five.

Social networks are two-way conduits. As well as transmitting information about jobs to the person searching for work they also transmit information in the opposite direction. They are the social channels through which the cultural capital of reputation enters the market-place and is conducted to specific sites within it. Cultural capital in the form of the reputation of both the sponsor and sponsored was important and is discussed later; and the beliefs and family routines which shaped and sustained individual and family reputations are taken up in the next chapter. However, since the asset of a reputation as a good worker, or as coming from a family with such a reputation, can only be realized in terms of a job if channels exist through which the information can flow, the number and quality of kinship and other affective links with the labour market mattered. The pattern of such links varied among individuals. Thus, although every young person in the study had kin of some kind who knew they would be looking for work on leaving school or when subsequently unemployed, these links with the labour market ranged from those in families where virtually no one was employed to those where all had work, as Figures 2.1 and 2.2 show. Such comparisons, however, still conceal the arbitrary nature of obtaining and retaining jobs.

At one extreme was Stuart Drake (Figure 2.1), unemployed after two spells as a YOP trainee, with a recently unemployed brother aged 20 and a stepfather in his fifties who had been unfit for work for over five years. His three sisters, married and living nearby in separate households, all had husbands who were unemployed. Only one of the sisters had a job, working part-time. Although other kin existed, and some aunts who lived away from the North-East visited the house from time to time, Stuart knew little about his relatives, commenting, 'I don't think there's any live round here. . . .I cannot *remember* none of them. . . .Never see them.' (emphasis in original).

In contrast, some young people were in regular contact with relatives employed in a wide range of occupations. Mark Freeman (Figure 2.2), an engineering apprentice since leaving school, lived in a household where everyone held a job. His father was a supervisor in a heavy engineering company, his mother worked part-time as an office cleaner in the shipyards and his older sister had a clerical job in the car trade. Four uncles worked in shipbuilding and heavy engineering, and five aunts were part-time cleaners and home helps. One male cousin was an engineering apprentice like himself, and another was currently doing casual, semi-skilled work, having been laid off on completion of his apprenticeship. A female cousin was not working because of illness when Mark was interviewed, but had previously held several jobs including one as a children's nanny working abroad.

While Mark had no kin at the firm where he was apprenticed, he had nonetheless been doubly advantaged by his contacts. He had been able to make a considered choice between the job his father had obtained for him and others where family contacts could vouch for his character. He said:

> Well, I had the choice of three jobs. . . .I did have a job at me Dad's place – he got us that, just about – . . . and . . . I turned that down. . . .I got an application form from the [ship] yards and . . . my uncle let us use his name for a . . . reference.

His father described how he had advised his son. 'I says, "Which d'you prefer?" He says, "I dunno." I says, "Well I think you'll probably get more experience at the engine works." . . . Because at my firm we just make components for . . . car engines. . . .'

An old family friend, Mr Oliver, a lifelong employee of the company, had supported Mark in his application for the job. Mark had named him on the application form which asked if he knew anyone who worked at the firm. Mr Freeman's account illustrates the transmission of reputation through affective channels at the interface of the private domain of family and friendship and the public domain of work:

> The personnel bloke had seen Mr Oliver at work and asked him what [Mark's] character was, what sort of lad he was y'know? . . . He got the job – I don't know whether it was through *that* – but that was a good recommendation (emphasis in original).

Nonetheless, success in finding a job seemed to be arbitrary. The two families described above appear to conform to the findings of those studies which suggest that unemployed people are more likely to come from families where other members are unemployed (Ashton and Maguire n.d.; Carroll 1979). Such observations, however, refer to aggregates. From the perspective of the individual, and for the people in the study, to be in a family where all were employed was neither a guarantee of employment nor protection against unemployment, as the following case illustrates.

Dawn Harris (Figure 2.2) had been unemployed for more than eighteen months after completing a YOP scheme, but had a whole

Figure 2.1 Contrasting employment statuses of kin for two unemployed young people

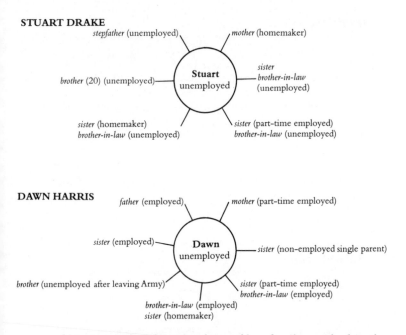

STUART DRAKE

stepfather (unemployed)

mother (homemaker)

brother (20) (unemployed)

Stuart unemployed

sister *brother-in-law* (unemployed)

sister (homemaker) *brother-in-law* (unemployed)

sister (part-time employed) *brother-in-law* (unemployed)

DAWN HARRIS

father (employed)

mother (part-time employed)

sister (employed)

Dawn unemployed

sister (non-employed single parent)

brother (unemployed after leaving Army)

sister (part-time employed) *brother-in-law* (employed)

brother-in-law (employed) *sister* (homemaker)

range of kin in steady jobs. Members of her family worked in the civil service (an older sister), for a finance company (a brother-in-law), and the local authority (her mother, in the school meals service). One older brother was unemployed after leaving the Army, but Dawn was the only other member of the kin network who could not find employment. Several of her relatives had offered Dawn practical help in her search for work without success. As Mrs Harris explained, 'Our Deirdre was able to tell us when [the] Ministry was interviewing, and *twice* we were able to get a form and go. She was able to help like that' (emphasis in original). Dawn's brother-in-law, she said,

> Did sometimes see . . . jobs, 'cos he's going in different shops . . . for the bank, and he'd come and say. . . .Nine times out of ten when she'd go, all *they* were interested in was the Youth Opportunity. . . .They didn't want to employ her because they'd have to pay her the full rate for the job (emphasis in original).

45

Figure 2.2 Contrasting employment statuses of kin for two employed young people

MARK FREEMAN

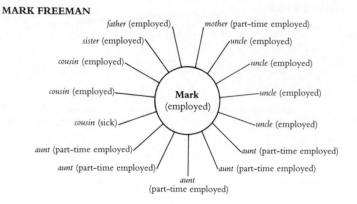

CAROLINE PRICE

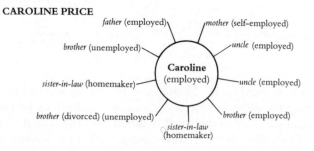

Conversely, young people from families where several members were unemployed could themselves be in work. Caroline Price (figure 2.2), for example, had been working for three years as a word-processor operator. A year previously her father had taken a poorly paid job as a cleaner after two months of unemployment following redundancy. His redundancy payment had been used to buy a small business which Mrs Price now ran, but which was bringing in only a tiny income. Two elder brothers had been unemployed for more than two years, while a third brother was in regular skilled work, employed by a motoring organization. She had two uncles who worked in the shipyards. None of her relatives had been involved in helping her get her job, which had started out as a YOP scheme, although one of her sisters-in-law had earlier worked for the same firm in a different department prior to being made redundant.

Moreover, whilst the experience of Mark Freeman (described above) was apparently conforming still to the stereotype of advantage, this image belies the reality emerging from a changing industrial base. The experience of his cousin, now employed in casual work despite completion of an apprenticeship, was not an isolated case and foreshadowed what was to happen to him by the end of the study if the report given by his relatives was correct. Once a guarantee of a steady trade and a passport to a secure future, apprenticeships – although still held in high esteem and dearly sought after by boys and their parents – could now be crowned by unemployment as the demand for these skills declined and as employers saw the advantages of replacing young men approaching the age of entitlement to 'full money' with younger, cheaper labour.

The changing and fragile quality of this social capital is reflected in the types of jobs and employment careers of those who had been successfully spoken for or who had heard of jobs through kin or friends of their own age (Table 2.3). Thirteen jobs had been obtained in this way, eight through kin. These openings had not been easily achieved despite the low level of skill required. For example, Mrs Bryant described how her husband had 'really pushed for their son', and Mr Hamilton said how he had 'pestered the life out of the personnel officer'. Others, like Stephen Woods, recounted their lack of success:

> [My mother] was gonna try and get us a start where she works, so was me brother and so was me dad, down their places. But they asked and there wasn't. They're still asking for us. My dad usually asks the gaffer of the place, 'cos me father gets on well with him.

Only one of these jobs had been an apprenticeship, which the boy had disliked. Because his college work was below standard he was laid off after a few months and offered unskilled work as an alternative. Another young man, David Robson, was labouring for a contractor and hence essentially insecure, whereas, as his mother pointed out, at one time her husband would have been able to press for jobs for his two sons within the firm itself. 'A few years ago, maybe, he could have put their names forward, but not now, they're just not starting people. But he's in touch with his contractors.' Moreover, of these jobs only three were still held at the

Table 2.3 Young people who were successfully 'spoken for' by kin or friends*

Name	Contact	Job	Status	Reason for leaving
Christine Dyer	Mother	Office junior	Full-time	Sacked after 1 month, typing below standard
Kathleen McGuinness	Friend	Snack-bar assistant	Part-time	Left because of conditions and obtained full-time work
" "	Sister-in-law	Clerk/receptionist	Full-time	Laid off after 3 months, lack of work
Andrew Black	Father	Labourer	Full-time	Laid off after 11 months, redundant, first in, last out
Andrew Black	Friend	Roofing labourer	Full-time	Still in post
Malcolm Bryant	Father	Labourer	Full-time	Still in post after 11 months
David Mitchell	Father	Apprentice, then labourer	Full-time	Still in post after 15 months
Philip Thompson	Father	Scaffolding worker	Temporary, full-time	Only lasted 3 weeks (only job he'd ever held), £140–190-a-week with overtime
Peter Hamilton	Friend	Glass collector	Part-time, later full-time	Low wages, joined YOP scheme
" "	Father	Labourer	Temporary	Full-Time, still in job after 3 months
David Robson	Father	Labourer for contractor		
Annette Maynard	Friend	Laundry worker	Full-time	Still in post
	Friend		Full-time	Resigned because of health
Margaret Hills	Friend	Catering assistant	Part-time, later full-time	Still in post

Note: * Mark Freeman is not listed here. He had not been 'spoken for' in the job he accepted although his reputation was 'checked'.

time of interview. Similarly, of the six jobs obtained through friends of their own age, only two were still held. The reasons for leaving reflect the fragility of the jobs. People left because of low wages (moving to a YOP scheme), for reasons of health, conditions of work and to take up a better job. The uncertainties and ambiguities encountered in this search for work led to a consideration of the situation and uncertainties young people met on finding a job of some kind, either on a government scheme or in paid employment.

INTO THE LABOUR MARKET

The experience of work itself, whether in paid employment or on YTS schemes, brought another set of disorientations. The poor and fluctuating labour market, where patterns of employment were changing and firms were as insecure as individuals, had several consequences for young people. There was a lowering of job aspirations from a level already realistically low, there was little certainty of being able to look forward to a continuous employment career – even less one with some advancement within it – many of the jobs and government schemes were seen as dead ends with no future if not outright exploitative, the norms governing the relationship between employer and employee seemed to be changing, and dilemmas arose for some in the temptation of small, illicit rewards from 'fiddle jobs' – low-paying jobs taken on a casual basis while also receiving state benefit.

Except for a few higher aspirations of the early teenage years, young people's ambitions had been modest; only a few had hoped to find employment in occupations where educational qualifications beyond CSE would be required. Just over half the young men (twelve) had hoped to obtain a craft apprenticeship and, through this, entry into skilled manual work, especially in engineering trades, joinery and car mechanics. Similar findings have been obtained in other studies of Newcastle upon Tyne; in one study, 64 per cent of boys in the city wanted apprenticeships when they left school (Youthaid 1981). However, only two of the Eldon boys gained apprenticeships and none of the others had been successful in obtaining the kind of work they wanted. At the time of interview, apart from Martin Pearce, the trainee auditing clerk who felt he had a job with prospects if he could hang onto it, the remainder were in labouring or other unskilled occupations, receiving no training, or were unemployed.

Not unexpectedly, the aspirations of the young women differed from those of the young men, reflecting the sexual divisions of the labour force (Hakim 1979). They had mostly hoped to obtain work in the traditional occupations for female workers on leaving school. The most popular ambitions were nursery nursing or other child-care work, clerical work and jobs as shop assistants. They had been a little more successful in realizing their ambitions than had the young men.

The modesty of these young people's jobs was reflected in their wages. At the age of 19 they took home weekly wages of between £40 and £60 (equivalent to £50 to £80 gross). This compares with average earnings in April 1984 of £82.30 for men aged 18 to 20 (New Earnings Survey, quoted by Lewis 1985). Lewis notes that nationally the lowest paid 10 per cent of men and women in this age group earned less than £62.10 and £58 weekly respectively. Those on YTS were getting £25 (topped up by some employers); those on supplementary benefit, £23.65 where they were 18 with no dependants.

Unlike their parents, these young people were entering a labour market in which it was difficult to carve out a steady employment career. In a buoyant economy this had been possible for parents and older brothers and sisters, even in low unskilled jobs, by always being in work, although not necessarily with the same employer; and it was an understood practice for people to opportunistically change jobs within the same sector for better pay and conditions. Mrs McGuire, for example, pointed out that until recently her older children, in a family of eleven, had never been out of work, 'not in the same job all the time, mind'. Some parents, in fact, had been able to work their way up in an organization, from labourer to supervisor, for example, like Mr Robson. Until two or three years prior to the study, few had gaps in their employment records and most displayed a pride in the continuity of their employment, a theme that is explored in the next chapter.

In contrast, sons and daughters in their late teens and early twenties, all wanting secure jobs, had entered a complex and changing scene. It was a labour market which encompassed extensive unemployment and varieties of paid work, including full-time, part-time, permanent and temporary employment, as well as the Youth Opportunities Programme (YOP) (Yeandle 1984). The uncertainties young people faced included the sheer arbitrariness of success or failure in obtaining work.

In this volatile situation, as noted earlier in the chapter, only seven of the young people had been continuously employed since leaving school, and not necessarily with the same employer; and although new jobs might be obtained before notice was worked out, to lose a job in a poor labour market could, as in the Pearce family, raise severe anxieties.

The rest had all had some experience of unemployment, some lasting more than two years. Those with no jobs to go to, or who had not found one soon after leaving school, had entered YOP schemes.

When YOP was first introduced in the 1970s, there was widespread expectation (fostered by central government) that it would ease the problems surrounding the extensive unemployment of school-leavers by providing a bridge between school and work. Many of the young people in the study took part in the programme with this in mind, but found that for them it was in reality a bridge to nowhere.[6]

Thirty-six of the forty young people in the study had held forty-six placements between them (Table 2.4). Few, only seven, had been able to convert their placement into a regular job, and these were not necessarily secure. Seventeen other young people had completed schemes but these had led either to further schemes or unemployment. Ten others had not completed the schemes for a variety of reasons.

Mr Bryant expressed vividly what many parents saw as a void facing young people when they left school and which, by their nature, schemes could not fill:

> They go all the way through the schooling system and all of a sudden there's nothing left for them. It's a dead end . . . a dead end. I think we must do our best to find some kind of real gainful employment for them. . . . I'm not talking about six months or twelve months schemes, they're not worth a light. I don't believe in the scheme, [and] I didn't like him being on it.

Here, as in other studies, (Coffield *et al.* 1986) the schemes were severely criticized both by participants and parents. Comments most frequently concerned the allowances paid (considered by many to be too low), the question of exploitation (slave labour was a term frequently used) and substitution of employees, the absence of adequate training, and the failure of YOP to lead to regular employment. A year after these interviews a report noted of

Table 2.4 Young people's participation in YOPs and outcomes

YOP outcomes	Females		Males		Total	
	Schemes*	Individuals[1]	Schemes*	Individuals[1]	Schemes*	Individuals[1]
Leading to employment	3	(3)	4	(4)	7	(7)
Completed but not leading to employment	11	(7)	12	(10)	23	(17)
Outcome unknown	0	(0)	3	(2)	3	(2)
Not completed	3	(3)	10	(7)	13	(10)
Total	17	(12)	29	(19)	46	(36)
Reason for Leaving						
Trainee found work	0	(0)	1	(1)	1	(1)
Firm closed	1	(1)	0	(0)	1	(1)
Trainee sacked	0	(0)	3	(3)	3	(3)
Dispute – left voluntarily	0	(0)	3	(3)	3	(3)
Other reasons – left voluntarily	2	(2)	3	(3)	5	(5)

Notes: * Some individuals fell into more than one category.
1. Numbers (in parentheses) of individuals moving between schemes.

YTS, which in 1983 replaced YOP, that 'in the North East, where unemployment is the worst in Britain', figures for the period from April 1985 to January 1986 showed that 'the proportion getting a job after YTS is just 44% – exactly the same as the proportion who join the dole queue' (Lewis 1986: 4).

Yet some 'proper' jobs were seen as even less satisfactory. Indeed, in one case, a job was relinquished in order to enter a YOP scheme in the hope of receiving some training. Peter Hamilton, a glass collector earning £44 a week in a club, remarked, 'I couldn't just stay a pot lad forever', thus intimating not only a notion about the level of income deemed appropriate but also a sense of what counted as a proper adult job. Jobs were futures. Mrs Potter, the mother of another who also resigned his job, explained, 'He got a job as a barman, just behind the bar, for about three months or something. But, you see, the money was no good.'

For both employed and unemployed the world of employment was one of uncertainty, paradox and irrationality. The uncertainties of the labour market were reflected in the collective experience of the group since leaving school at the ages of 16 or 17 (Table 2.5). Thirteen had never held a job apart from participation in a government scheme. Of the remaining twenty-seven who had secured jobs, only seven had been continuously employed; the other twenty had suffered spells of unemployment of varying lengths. Between them, these twenty-seven young people had held forty-three jobs: seventeen had held one job of varying duration, whilst ten young people accounted for the rest, many of them of short duration.

Job-changing by young people in the unskilled sector of the labour market is a recognized way of securing better jobs; the

Table 2.5 Number of jobs held by young people since leaving school

No. of jobs	No. of jobs		
	Females	Males	Total
0	5	8	13
1	9	8	17
2	1	3*	4
3 or more	2*	4*	6
Total	17	23	40

Note: * The figures include some part-time jobs.

movement here, however, was occurring at a time when people generally felt that to have a job, however poor or hated, was more likely to be a stepping-stone to something better than was unemployment. Significantly, a substantial number of the reasons given for leaving jobs – expiry of contract, being laid off, leaving part-time work – reflects more the condition of the labour market than individual idiosyncrasies. Ashton and Maguire reached similar conclusions: that this pattern of job movement is 'more adequately explained by the level of activity in the economy and the segment of the labour market first entered by young adults' (Ashton and Maguire n.d.: 157).[7]

Thus while Phillips (1973) identified job-changing, or simply leaving jobs which were disliked for any reason, as characteristic of young workers, in a climate of high unemployment some young people held onto poorly paid or otherwise unattractive jobs whilst searching for other work. As Bryan Jones observed of his job as a storeman: 'It wasn't the one I wanted, like, but I couldn't get the one I wanted. I've been looking for another job for the last eighteen months now, since I started there, and I'm still drawing blank.' The strategy was realistic in a society where employment status colours perceptions of ability and character. 'He says, "While you've got a job it's much easier to get another", which is true,' said Mrs Pearce of her son who had now moved to a new position, able now to leave the one where he had been treated as a 'dog's body'. The comment reflects the damaging image the status of unemployment bestows upon the individual.

Such a strategy, however, is dependent upon having a job in the

Table 2.6 Duration of jobs held and outcome

	Duration					
Outcome	Less than 1 month	1–3 months	4–6 months	7–12 months	More than 1 year	Total
Job still held	–	1	3	4	12	20
Laid off	–	2	-	1	2	5
Sacked	2	1	2	-	1	6
Left voluntarily	1	5	1	-	1	8*
Contract expired	1	2	-	1	-	4
Total	4	11	6	6	16	43

Note: * This figure includes one where duration was unknown and four part-time jobs.

first place. Jobs were scarce. Moreover, even for those in work such a plan could be irrelevant since obtaining or losing a job seemed to be quite arbitrary. 'Hanging on' until something better was found was not in the control of the employee. Irrespective of whether it had been held for years, months or weeks, a job could be brought to an abrupt end by the changing structure of the labour market, the sudden demise of a firm and the increase in contract work and temporary employment, as Kathleen McGuinness found when the travel firm in which her sister-in-law had found her a job folded after three months. Others were on temporary work and lived with the knowledge of its insecure future. For those who had entered the apprenticeship system or knew people in it, the contrast with the former security this system offered highlighted the new situation. For not only had several young people experienced short-term and temporary work, but those in what had once been the epitome of secure steady employment could face the same fate. Bryan Jones' cousin, Martin Rice, was doing semi-skilled work on temporary contracts after being laid off on completing his training as a craft apprentice. Through his cousin, Bryan, who was working as a storekeeper for take-home pay of less than £40 per week, had put his name down at the same firm, but was aware of the ephemeral character of the job. As Bryan said, 'You can get laid off *any* time, there. It's temporary work and it's good *money*, but they can just lay you off *any* time, maybe four, five weeks and then take you on again' (emphasis in original).

Thus what had seemed a good start turned into a dead end. There was an air of waiting and suspense surrounding such experiences, evident in Mr Rice's comments about his elder son's period out of work and his present casual job. 'Until such time as he gets a full-time job at his trade, . . . this job'll serve – although it'll be temporary, and sometimes he's laid off for a week or half a week – until his trade picks up again.'

This restructuring labour market enhanced the power of employers to the disadvantage of their workers, particularly the young. Power has to be constantly negotiated to be sustained (Molotoch 1975) and there was evidence that the labour market norms governing the relationship between employer and employee were being renegotiated.[8] This sense of unwelcome change was reflected in comments ranging from the apparently trivial to more serious threats concerning pay and conditions of work. It appeared in the complaints about lack of common decency, politeness and feeling when letters of application, which could be an arduous and costly exercise, were not answered. Similarly there was a sense of unfairness, as well as anxiety and uncertainty, when people were not told until the last minute whether or not they were to be kept on following a YOP placement with a firm, or in a temporary job when there was a possibility of it becoming permanent. Also condemned was the growing practice of finishing an apprentice before his time was served, or of replacing people with younger, cheaper labour when they reached an age-related wage level. And the personal resource of 'being a hard worker' used in the competition to be 'kept on' was outweighed by the cost to the employer.

This is not to say that such practices were new, but the power of the employee to influence them was in retreat. Condemnation, therefore, was tempered with caution about the wisdom of pressing employers too far in pursuit of what were seen as rights, a theme which is developed in later chapters. Thus whilst there were complaints about low levels of pay for a good day's work, there was a hesitancy on the part of some parents to intervene, or to encourage their children to clarify their position with an employer, or to press for better conditions in case it led to loss of the job. Mr Johnson described the problem:

> At first it was something for him to *do* rather than just lie around the house, but *now* I look at it as a bit of a career for him. He's getting low wages, I divent like it, but I don't want to jump in because I can go up there and say to them, 'That's not quite enough,' and then he'll say, 'Well, I divent want him.' But when he does reach twenty-one he's entitled to a full carpet-fitting rate, he might even be thinking of starting his own house – place, which is good, but you can't do that unless they treat you right. When he's reached twenty-one he's got to decide whether he pushes it for the full rate of pay (emphasis in original).

Awareness of change extended beyond the formal sector of the labour market into the informal sector of 'fiddle-jobs', those jobs undertaken on a casual and informal basis when drawing state benefit and usually offering low pay. Evidence about 'fiddling' or 'scrounging' has failed to support the view that the practice is widespread (Marsden 1982), but many here thought it was extensive.

Two strands ran through the views expressed. First, some attitudes were coloured by a sense of moral decline. Fiddling was felt to be wrong. This could stem from it being seen as dishonest, as unfair to those who work for all their income, as reducing the number of proper jobs by undercutting the market, or because it increased the taxes of those in work. It was felt that standards were being eroded both by those who accepted such work and by those who offered it. In contrast, however, there were those who approved; but it was an approval that could be accompanied by dilemma. This period of the life course, before full adulthood and settling down, was a time when after making a contribution to household expenses and covering their personal needs, young people were expected to have at least a small amount of spare cash so that they could 'go out and enjoy themselves'. Consequently, since the amount of state benefit a young person was entitled to was so low, and the income disregard[9] of £4 a week so little, to earn a small supplement did not seem unreasonable. Several parents and young people felt that the regulations should be changed.[10]

As the situation stood, however, the legal restrictions created personal and family dilemmas, producing what Wilensky (1969:129) has called 'expedient conformity'.[11] Thus young people refused offers of such jobs (and such offers were few) because of the fear of getting into trouble. People were convinced that if they accepted a fiddle job it would be 'just their luck to be caught', and some parents, for the same reason, counselled their children against taking these jobs or refused to allow them to take them. Fiddle jobs in such 'hard times' thus provoked dilemmas for both the individual and the family. Anxiety and worry would not be confined to the person doing the job, and there was the problem of advising a son or daughter over a regulation which was deemed to be in need of change; it was a legal rather than a moral restriction which directed behaviour. These dilemmas and the shifting moral ground which fed into the concerns about young people's futures are discussed in Chapter Four from the perspective of order in people's lives.

CONCLUSION

This chapter has described the complexities of the immediate effects of a restructing labour market upon young people and their families. The focus has been upon change and uncertainty in the labour market itself, the repercussions upon the employment careers of young adults and the way families responded to these changes. This provides the familial context for later chapters which show in detail how such changes penetrate family life.

The changes induced by the labour market were examined in three ways: first, the many and unpredictable changes in family employment statuses; second, the effect of labour-market change upon family resources and the deployment of these resources in the search for work; and third, young people's experience in the labour market and the apparent changes in practices and expectations governing work conditions and relationships.

The changing and uncertain labour market produced kaleidoscopic changes in the employment statuses of family members as they unpredictably gained and lost jobs. Although one young person in each family was central to the study, his or her experience could not be understood in isolation from what was happening to other family members and the uncertainty and anxiety which the seemingly arbitrary changes brought.

The second part of the chapter looked at the search for work. Here the emphasis was upon the resources young people and their families could draw upon in this search. Resources, of course, varied amongst individuals and families, but again a picture of change and uncertainty emerged as some, both parents and young people, discovered how the changes in the labour market undermined and devalued some resources and put severe strain upon others. Thus qualifications did not guarantee a job, few government schemes provided training leading to permanent jobs, and the difficulties experienced by a hard-pressed careers service and the rules operating in some job centres led to anomalies which seemed to contradict the pressures upon and desire for work amongst young people.

Family resources of time, emotion and finance were used to sustain a work ethic, sometimes leading to strain and disruption of family relationships – an issue taken up in later chapters. The situation also revealed that resources do not stand in isolation from each other if goals are to be achieved. Thus economic resources allowed the individual to cut a swath through some regulations and thus use their cultural capital vested in state job centres in a flexible way. Access to appropriate social networks was necessary for the cultural capital of reputation to be fed into the labour market. As the traditional industrial base declined, so did such networks, and the resources of those who had been geared to them dissolved. Resources could also critically link the private and public domains of family and labour market, blurring the distinction frequently made between formal and informal methods of finding work. For example, economic parental subsidies of bus fares gave access to the state careers service; and the affective support in accompanying a daughter to an interview meant that by actually arriving she at least was in the running for a job.

The third strand of labour market change was associated with the norms which governed the relationship between employers and employees. Here the focus was upon young people's experience of work, whether in employment or on government schemes. There was a sense of exploitation accompanied by fears over the outcome of any challenge as power in the labour market increasingly favoured the employer. There was disillusionment when hard work and commitment did not necessarily retain a job when in competition with replacement cheap labour. There were also the diverse views raised by the possibility of casual earnings whilst drawing state benefit. Here there was the contrast between the moral disapproval of some and, for others, the dilemma posed by the fear of being caught breaking the law whilst feeling that supplementing low state benefits in this way was quite reasonable.

Both these positions were influenced by cultural expectations about the character of the transitional years of young adulthood. The effect of the recession upon young people's developing independence during these years, in the context of family relationships, is the subject of the next chapter.

3

INDEPENDENCE AND
WORK

INTRODUCTION

Littler (1985) has observed that despite the continued rise in unemployment through the 1970s and 1980s, there is little evidence of decline either in the significance most people attach to paid work or in the stigma attached to unemployment. Some have drawn attention to the continuing resilience of the work ethic[1] amongst a wide range of social groups. This is not to suggest that large sections of the population hold a precise understanding of the behaviour patterns and values which Weber propounded as components of the ethic – ascetism, hard work, the morality of work itself, frugality, not being idle, the notion that time is money and so forth. But as Brock (1985) notes when discussing Furnham's work on attitudes towards the unemployed, 'It is enough to know that the "feel" (rather than a precise understanding) of the ethic is still strong in people's minds'.

This study not only lent support to this view, it also highlighted, within the context of family life, the part played by beliefs about paid work and the role of paid work in a person's transition from the dependency of childhood to the independence of adulthood.

As noted earlier, youth is not a unitary concept and, under the influences of class, ethnicity and gender, routes to independence can take a variety of forms. Whatever the route, however, independence is symbolized by leaving home and setting up an independent household, and, as Morgan has pointed out, 'marriage is seen as being identified with the attainment of full adult status . . . with settling down' (Morgan 1977: 183). The young people and the parents in the Newcastle study were at that stage in their family cycle when such considerations were either present or on the

60

horizon. Their day-to-day lives intimately centred on those events, punctuating these years, which are seen as leading to independence and which are deeply affected by the state of the labour market.

In the private domain of the family the links between paid work and independence are cultural, social and economic. First, beliefs about paid work and independence have deep cultural and social roots in family life; they do not suddenly emerge with the end of full-time education and entry into the labour market. Because of the decisions which have to be made and steps which have to be taken during these few years of adolescence and early adulthood, the two themes of work and independence are more visible at this juncture of the life course than in the earlier years. They are, however, part of the substance of parenting and, in the socialization of the child and young person, reach back into the early years of infancy. Ideas about work and independence are, moreover, not confined to overt prescription and advice but are embedded in the family discourse of everyday life – that is, in the interaction which takes place between family members at many levels. They inform, for example, household routines and rules, the exchange of services, money and gifts; they are implicit and explicit in duties and obligations; and are part of imagery and metaphor upon which people draw to describe, explain and order their lives (Salmon 1985). Through such familial discourse this aspect of cultural capital is transmitted – not unproblematically, because the process itself is one of negotiation – to the next generation, shaping identities and reputations.

Second, from 'having a job' a person derives cultural, economic and social capital which can be converted into other forms of power. For the majority of young people, independence unfolds whilst living in the parental home, within an established pattern of family relationships, but to achieve independence these relationships must be renegotiated. Unlike some other cultures, there are no initiation rites which mark the entry into adulthood; in our society the status of adulthood is partly ascribed and partly achieved. Thus while the mere facts of reaching certain ages and leaving school are generally recognized by parents and children as heralding new stages and changes in the relationship between the generations, paid employment, signifying the achieved status of worker, endows the young adult with added power to renegotiate rights, duties and obligations with parents and siblings.

This chapter looks at the roots of independence in family life, especially at how they are articulated with the theme of work, and at the effect of a poor labour market upon relationships within the family during this transitional stage to independence. A third aspect – the effect of a poor labour market upon the order and sequencing of events in the progression to independence and 'settling down' – is touched upon here but addressed in more detail in the next chapter.

THE FAMILIAL ROOTS OF INDEPENDENCE

Independence is a dominant value in our culture. It is not, however, merely the outcome of an innate developmental process but an important component of parenting, purposely encouraged and nurtured. In her study of early parenthood, Backett found that 'the notion of independence did not suddenly emerge in the late teens with the entry into work. Even in the early stages from babyhood onwards, there were notions of "freedom" and "letting go"' (Backett 1982: 25). This was echoed by Mrs Pearce in the Newcastle study, who observed of her son, when he was a compliant 8-year-old, 'It used to worry me at the back of my mind. I used to think, "He's not naughty enough . . . there's something wrong"'; and she outlined the strategies she had used to encourage self-reliance.[2] Such encouragement, although obviously subject to changes as the child grows older, is not confined to the childhood years but continues over the threshold of early adulthood into the world of work. Thus, although leaving school may herald a change in the relationship between parents and their children, independence is still not left to take its own course.

Independence from parents, culminating in the establishment of an independent household, is a deeply held expectation for both generations. It would be deemed a failure in parenting if this, in some form, were neither achieved nor encouraged. In the Newcastle study this was sharply felt even by those who would feel a great wrench or loss. The following reflects not only this acceptance of a cultural norm but the unanticipated ache and anxiety created by recession. Of her daughter, who got a job in the South, one mother said,

> It's no good saying I didn't mind, I did mind. I didn't want her to go. I don't want any of mine to leave home . . . but the time's going to come . . . when they are. But to leave home to get married is to lead a new life. To go away because you've

got to work . . . is a worry because you don't know whether they're going to get work . . . permanent work, or not.

(Mrs Rice)

Parental expectations about independence were echoed in remarks made by young people. Although some young people said that they had always been given a sense of independence by their parents, as noted earlier, there was certainly a feeling that certain rights and privileges accrued with age – for example, freedom in the selection of friends and times of coming home at night. Age was also associated with the sense of there being an appropriate time for leaving 'the nest'. 'I don't want to leave home – I just feel I *should*, that it's about time', observed one young woman (emphasis in original). Sometimes reflected in such comments was a sense of obligation not to burden parents: 'They don't want me hanging round their necks' (Karen Hughes).

Awareness that adjustments were being made by both parties was evident. That a dialogue between the generations was taking place is clear in the following quotation:

> They're learning to understand now, that at my age it's about time I left the family nest [and] learn to live on my own, depend on myself and things like that. Then they learned to understand what I meant.

(Christine Dyer)

Parents and children were conscious that the legitimacy which enabled parents to impose certain rules was receding. Parents were now having to trust the efficacy of their teachings and the extent to which they had inculcated a sense of responsibility in their children. As Mrs Pearce recounted,

> I think a lot of my ways have rubbed off onto. . . . 'You must do this and you haven't got to do that sort of thing' [laughs]. But we were talking about it the other day and I says, 'You – you wouldn't do anything I didn't want you to do?' He says, 'Mam, if I thought it was right and I wanted to do it, yes, I would.' And I was taken aback because . . . now I've realized he *is* growing up. I know he's 19. You don't realize they're growing up and you still expect them to do as you. . . .It was a shock and I was taken aback. I thought, 'Ee', you know, 'I-I'm not . . . boss any more' [laughs] (emphasis in original).

63

In this changing power relationship the young adults also recognized how easily parental injunctions could be evaded. As Margaret Hills observed,

> I mean, if you get as far as the interview stage and didn't want the job, you can literally say, 'Well, I don't want this job, I'm being forced into it.' Come home and say, 'I didn't get it' [laughs]. If you're being – having pressure put on you.

The effect of the recession on these sensitive, and for some difficult, adjustments was marked and is discussed later. Suffice it to say that when a young person could not obtain paid employment both parties could suffer. The young lost the power bestowed by an earned income to renegotiate their place in the family; parents could find their authority implicitly undermined when their advice proved ineffective or inappropriate to a poor labour market.

THE COMPONENTS OF INDEPENDENCE

Self-reliance

Independence was not only expected but also anticipated, and this assumption that a child would eventually leave home coloured the practices and routines of family life. Thus, while independence was seen as good in itself, as a personal quality, as having a mind of one's own and a sense of responsibility, also seen as important was self-sufficiency, the ability to manage by oneself.

For example, one of the motifs which ran through the issue of a child's involvement in domestic tasks, an involvement which was highly variable,[3] was not so much the sharing of the domestic burden but the development of self-reliance. This is not to deny that feelings about fairness and injustice occurred, but they were not central to the issue of independence. The crucial point was the ability to perform domestic tasks successfully. This, it was felt, could and should be taught in the home as preparation for when offspring left, or for the times when parents were unable to service them. To this end it was not necessary that children undertake domestic tasks in any regular or committed fashion; children had merely to demonstrate that they could perform them if necessary. Parents' dismay at the domestic incompetence and disinterest shown by some children sustained this interpretation.

Against this background, the elements out of which such independence was to be constructed included clearly recognizable elements of the work ethic, particularly the notion of work itself, the value of money and the discipline of time. It was around these themes that an approved kind of independence was articulated. The different kinds of independence are discussed in Chapter Four.

The value of money

By definition homes had an economic ambience. Although, in some parents' opinions, concern about money did not always transfer itself to their children in the manner they would have wished, some children grew up in an atmosphere of tight and conscious money management. It was present in the homes of both the employed and the unemployed young people, and in homes where all members were in work as well as those where all were out of work.

In a family of three where all worked and none had been unemployed, apart from that caused by her recent industrial injury, Mrs Pearce, for example, had a complicated system of money boxes by which she regulated her various financial commitments. Similarly, Mrs Kelly, the mother of a family where the stepfather and all the children were unemployed, described a rigorous system of monetary control, allocating parts of the fortnightly income from different state benefits to different purses, putting one purse away in a disciplined fashion because, as she observed of her own economic weaknesses, 'money burnt a hole' in her purse. Her children's contribution to the household in board money, paid out of their state benefit, and the child benefit for her younger child, were tightly integrated into this system. Her unemployed son paid the highest amount of board money – £15 – of the group studied. She, like others, had had to balance the losses and gains in children's benefit payments, unemployment benefit and social security as her children left school. She expected and received (with the approval of the young person interviewed) board money from her unemployed children equivalent to the state benefits lost to her household income when the children left school.[4]

Other signs of money management showed in the careful shopping procedures of several families, cutting across all the employment groupings. It appears, for example, in the practice of travelling across the city for a cheaper weekly family shop, in buying clothes that would last, or in restricting buying and limiting entertainment in order to stay within means. Some, like Mr Johnson, the father in a family of three wage-earners, referred to a well-recognized philosophy of 'Working, saving, spending . . . because that's the way I believe it should be . . . save a bit and spend a bit'. As Mr Fox pointed out, 'Trying to make them have some sense where money's concerned' was seen as a key part of a parent's role – to learn its value, to develop a sense of priorities (not to buy a music centre before a washing machine like the young couple next door, for example) and to learn how to manage it.

Although Mrs Pearce referred to her 'ways rubbing off' onto her son, and Mrs Hughes, for instance, felt that important economic aspects of a 'parents' job' were performed 'by example, more than anything else', there were conscious attempts to develop habits which would last a lifetime. One way of orientating children to the value of money was through the habit of saving. Several parents encouraged saving from an early age, but this encouragement became more widespread as children started work. It was, of course, circumscribed by a family's economic circumstances; some felt themselves to be too poor to encourage it. The range of practices adopted extended from the money boxes of young children to insurance premiums (usually paid by parents) as they grew older, the use of banks and building societies and parental approval of employers' savings arrangements whereby a regular sum was deducted from wages at source. Parents sometimes acted as 'bankers' taking their child's money to the bank, or gave them 'a start', as did Mr Fox:

> I opened a small bank account for 'im. Just started one off, about 12 months ago. I says, 'There you are. There's your start. . . .It's up to you now to keep . . . putting a little bit in, even if it's only a pound or two a week,' I said. 'It soon builds up. You look after the pennies, the pounds'll look after theirselves.'

Parents also gave solicited and unsolicited financial advice. Again Mr Fox's account reveals not only the early and persistent attempts at guidance which continued into early adulthood, but nicely illustrates the connections between independence, money and work. It also reveals how parental knowledge became meaningful to a son or daughter when it coincided with a relevant set of circumstances in their own life course.

To try and find out what the *value* of money is, you know,
. . . because . . . if he's got money it burns a bloody hole in
his pocket, you know. I think it probably does to most people.
But I try to say to him, 'Now look, try and live as though you
were livin' on your *own*, in a *flat* of your own. You're gettin' X
number of pounds a week. And sit *down*, and just think what it
would *cost* you just for your food alone a week. For example,
you buy a box of cornflakes, you've got to buy eggs, you've
got to buy bacon, you've got to put a little bit away for your
gas, a little bit away for your electric,' I said. 'Now tot that all
up,' I said. 'You've got to end up with a job *somewhere* bringin'
you in about £50–£55 a week, for you to live *reasonable*,' yer
know. 'Well, no, *that's* all a load of rubbish, Dad, all a load
of rubbish.' And now since he *started* work, . . . he started
to *realize* now exactly what the value of money is. And the
daughter's the same, you know, it – but we try and tell her
an' that, two or three years ago. It just went in one ear and
straight out the other (emphasis in original).

In this weaning and constructing process the function of board
money was educational. On this point some parents were extremely
vociferous, like Mrs Matthews who denounced as failing in their
parental duty those who neither insisted upon, nor expected, some
financial contribution from their economically active children,
whether in work or unemployed. Others regretted their earlier
indulgence on the matter.[5] This is not to say that board money
covered the full economic cost of the child, and, as has been
found in other studies of young people, this was recognized
by both young people and their parents (Leonard 1980; Wallace
1987). An economic balance was not expected, however. Indeed,
some young people received more from their parents in pocket
money than they handed over as 'board'. And, while Mrs Pearce
could itemize in detail the subsidies to her son – even down to
his girlfriend's tea – she not only recounted her own father's
one hurtful remark when she told him she was getting married
– that they had 'not had anything out of her yet' – but she was
also saving her son's board money to return to him as a lump
sum on his own marriage. Mrs Jones, moreover, in her worry
about her daughter seeking work away from home, highlighted
how necessary parental subsidies were, especially when jobs were
scarce.

Well it was just sort of her like going away from home. I know she was quite capable and trustworthy and that . . . but it was just if she didn't get a job. *How* would she manage on her dole money and that, because when they are at home they get treats and different things (emphasis in original).

The essential nature of these 'treats and things' was starkly apparent in one case. Although as Mrs Hughes said, 'Once you leave school you're on your own, . . . you've got to be an adult,' there are degrees of independence. Without parents you literally were on your own. Neil Peters, a 19-year-old orphan sharing a flat with a friend, had been independent since leaving a children's home at 16 years of age. His malnutrition and the abject poverty in which he lived, the absence of parental support and counselling, drew attention to the critical role of parents during the years of young adulthood. As he said, 'Well, some people you see get their own flat. But they still got their mothers to run to if they ever get any problems, whereas I haven't.' Wallace's (1987) interviews with young people on Sheppey suggest that this practice is widespread.

The transfers were not solely in one direction – that is, from parents to children. Parents would 'get it back in kind', and in the affection of their children. However, that it was a weaning process can be inferred from the gentle nudge towards an increased household contribution following a pay rise made by one mother, 'Do I get a rise, too?' The purpose of these transfers is well summarized by Paul Lewis:

The net transfer of money and goods in both directions between parents and a child is the means by which the young person is taught about the obligations as well as the freedom of adulthood life while the parent continues to provide goods and services.

(Lewis 1985: 5)

The ethos of work

Notions about self-reliance and money were underpinned and mediated by the concept of work. Since the subject of work and unemployment was at the heart of the study, which was undertaken when jobs were difficult to get, not unexpectedly talk of work was a dominant theme in the interviews. What was surprising, however, was the pervasiveness of the theme. Thus, playing a subtle role in the shaping of independence was the way beliefs about work infused language, thinking and family routines.

In these interviews people gratuitously defined themselves and others in terms of work: their families, mothers, fathers, daughters, sons, siblings, kin and people in general. People were proud of the fact that they had always been in work, that they were willing to work, and if unemployed, explained why they couldn't work – it might, for example, be due to a parent's sickness or to a young person's criminal record. 'I've always worked', or 'I've never been out of work', were frequent statements. Attention was drawn to the morality of working – for example, how a husband or a child worked when chronically sick or unwell.

Mr Hughes said he had never 'lost a day's work. . . .I've never consciously thought . . . about having a day off to go on the skive.' He referred to his daughter who'd had a day or so off with a cold as the only one in the family 'leant that way', as though it were a deviant tendency built into the character:

> Actually there's none of me kids ever wanted to take a day off work. Whether it come from me or not I divent know. Karen's the only one that's ever . . . had a day off work I think. Even then it's only . . . maybe once, twice a year. But she's the only one that's . . . ever . . . leant that way at all, you know.

The depth of the theme was reflected in the way it recurred in both insults and worries, and amongst employed and unemployed. An ex-boy friend was remembered by one young woman as a lay-about, and a former son-in-law as one who 'would neither work nor want'. A mother worried about her daughter's choice of friends because 'they seemed as if they didn't want to work', while another described her daughter's friend as 'a good little worker'. Children were respected by their parents for 'sticking' at low-paid jobs. 'When he's in a job,' said Mr Jones, 'he's prepared to work hard. . . .Something you've got to be prepared to do . . . if you want to make a living.'

In a tautological way the importance of being a good worker found expression the attributes of character and behaviour of which it was seen to consist. Along with working hard went reliability and good timekeeping. Mr Hewitt, when asked if his ability to obtain work was due to luck, replied:

Well . . . I wouldn't say luck, I mean – I've always been a good *worker*, you know a good *time*keeper and that. . . .My son's always been the same . . . he never loses any time unnecessarily like. In fact, I cannot remember the last time I lost a quarter,[6] yer know when I've been late for work. . . .I cannot really remember that, it must be years and years ago (emphasis in original).

One mother, who could not persuade her daughter to stay at home when sick, reported her as saying, 'Oh, I'll have to go. . . .I couldn't let people down like that.' (Mrs Hughes)

Comments about work and its relationship to money could be strongly moral in tone. Thus the source of income – that is, from paid work as opposed to state benefit – irrespective of the amount, could influence both the perception of its value and the worthiness of the recipient.

Suppose you only work for coppers . . . you've *worked* for it. I mean you go to the dole, it's something off the government for nowt. You don't *value* that – but when you work for it, you say, 'I've earned that money, I've deserved it.' It's not summat for nowt. It's like charity, the dole. It's like begging (emphasis in original).

(Mr Page)

This moral theme and its material effects upon relationships are returned to later in the chapter.

The inculcation of such traits was not confined to exhortation but firmly located in household routines. The clearest was the family's role in industrial timekeeping. There are many interdependencies of family schedules and the schedules of industrial organizations.[7] The example used here is that of the family getting off to school and work each morning. Mr Hewitt contrasted the good timekeeping observed by his children with the difficulties experienced by some parents:

You might hear people talking about when they get their kids up for work and they've got to shout five and six times to get them up. Well I get up first . . . about quarter past six . . . and I just open her [his daughter's] door, . . . just shout her name like . . . about half past six [she's] up. We never have any problem.

This task, however, most frequently fell to the wife – mother. Even when others took over, as in Mr Hewitt's case, it was implicitly seen as someone undertaking duties culturally ascribed to her.[8] Mrs Jones' description, when asked about her usual daily routine, echoes that of many mothers: 'Starting from getting up . . . putting up [sandwiches] for my husband . . . and waking them up . . . I normally get up at six o'clock . . . and I normally get *them* up at ten to seven' (emphasis in original). The diary she kept for one day, for the purposes of the study, provided the detail:

6 a.m.: get up, went downstairs, put kettle on, put husband's lunch up, woke son up with cup of tea.
7 a.m.: put kettle on, had a cup of coffee, woke husband with a cup of tea, got ready for work.
8 a.m.: woke daughter up for work, made bed.
8.30 a.m.: washed dishes, went to work.

This industrial patterning of family life, and the dilemmas raised by unemployment, could be traced in the anxieties and tensions amongst parents and young people over the issue of 'staying in bed' and late rising when people were out of work. It is a complex phenomenon and is discussed later in this chapter and in the following one.

People drew a direct link between work and money. It was exemplified by the comment of one young man, 'If you want to eat you've got to work.' The connection was also implicit in both critical and conventional observations on the social and financial benefits of schoolchildren's part-time jobs.[9] Some parents criticized the unrealistic nature of these jobs, which demanded neither commitment nor responsibility. Mr Howard observed, 'They don't put their mind to it, they only earn a few pennies. You work to keep yourself, whereas a Saturday job is for pocket money.' In contrast, others emphasized the value of this early entry into the labour market because of the 'insight it gave into . . . how they've got to make a living . . . [and] just how hard money is to come by'. There were also comments which revealed the independence and power such income bestowed, and again hinted at the moralities surrounding earned income, a theme introduced even prior to full entry into the labour market:

They've got a little bit of pocket money of their own which they can say, 'It's my pocket money, I've worked for it.' So if they want to buy something they can go out and say, 'Well, I've saved the money and I bought it myself.'

(Mrs Johnson)

MacLennan *et al.*, from a survey of 1700 working schoolchildren conducted in 1982–83, observed that equally central to the conventional view of children's labour is the perception of such employment as not only a healthy pastime (unlike earlier child labour) encouraging responsibility and bestowing a degree of financial freedom, but also 'the notion that the discipline of the labour market is a good thing, even for children' (MacLennan *et al.* 1985: 1). Parents in the Newcastle study were well aware of the harsh realities of work which their children had to learn. As one mother observed, 'He comes in shattered. He's been made to realize that working is not a bed of roses.' That both grind and moralities were somehow inherent in working was evident. 'There must be better ways of life than having to work for a living, as long as you keep it legal,' said Mr Hills; and a deep-seated work imperative was clearly expressed by Mr Freeman: 'I don't enjoy work, but I just think I shouldn't sort of skive. . . .'

The help offered and pressure placed upon children to seek work were discussed in the last chapter. These are raised again here as aspects of parental duty, whose importance is shown by an instance where this pressure was consciously abandoned. Many parents emphasized the need these days to 'be a bit pushy'. 'Unless *you* put *yourself* out to *go* and look for things', said Mr Fox, referring to the current practice whereby young people were no longer notified of vacancies by employment agencies,

I think you're gonna be a person who could probably end up on the dole for the rest of your bloody life. That's not *me*, I've been a working man all my life, you know, and that's how I try to put it over to *them* (emphasis in original).

The sentiment was echoed by others. 'Today', said Mrs McGuinness, referring to the poorer employment opportunities, 'You had to be a bit pushy. . . .Things don't just drop into your lap, you've got to go out and be a bit pushy.' And Mrs McGuire, while sympathizing with her three unemployed daughters and aware of the contrast with her own youthful experience, nonetheless felt that individual effort was still necessary:

> I think if they *tried* a little bit *harder* they *might* be lucky and get a job. . . .I keep saying '*You* should, *you* should have a job, *you* should have a job' (indicating the three girls not present). When I was young. . . .' 'Oh, mother, you're not going to start again? When you were young there was jobs.' I says, 'Yes, but you still had to make the *effort* . . . to go *after* these jobs' (emphasis in original).

She felt that her children had lost the incentive to work; she was, however, also aware of a moral imperative rather than one which was solely economic. They 'just didn't care' and 'don't feel . . . as if it's wrong not to work'.

In contrast, Mrs Kelly did not make any such demands of her son. She felt he had lost 'his instinct for work' because of the duration of his unemployment, the low pay of the work schemes for which he was eligible and the necessity to contribute a substantial proportion of his income to household finances:

> 'I'm not making you go to work son for £25 a week.' By the time they pay their bus fares and they pay their board (£15) they've nothing left . . . especially my bairns when having to pay me . . . the money I was losing off social security when they left school.

Parental duties included that of nurturing a sense of employment rights, sometimes stepping in to ensure them – for example, insisting on a reference for a son and standing in the office until it was received, or telephoning about the excessive hours for no extra pay a daughter was expected to work. In the context of the present discussion, these illustrate not just a parental protectiveness which extended into the labour market, but also show how parents teach an understanding of workers' rights. It was also noted in the last chapter, however, how the poor condition of the labour market could infringe both rights and the ability to challenge such infringements. The concepts of rights and duties as components of full citizenship and the effects of economic recession upon the processes through which citizenship is given meaning are discussed later.

The chapter so far has concentrated upon how ideas about work and independence have a history which is deeply rooted in family life. The next part of the chapter shows how a poor labour market affects young people's negotiation of independence within the family.

PAID EMPLOYMENT

Families provided young people with an orientation to the world of work and the rudiments of independence whilst children were still fully dependent; and even on leaving school, and with access to an independent income, independence was still seen by parents as in need of careful nurturing and direction. The young were considered vulnerable, for there is more than one road to independence, a theme described in more detail in the next chapter. In brief, a child might develop 'a taste' for what was considered to be an unsuitable way of life. Concern for the child's future, therefore, dictated that independence should be of an approved kind, one which held the promise that adult responsibilities could eventually be undertaken. To live 'decent' or 'reasonable' connotes in the first instance an acceptable standard of living for the individual but, second, one which eventually (especially for the males in the study) enables them to support a family. This concern was revealed in the responses of parents and young people when talk was of marriage, living on the 'social', poverty and the moralities surrounding waged work, burglary and crime as sources of income. It related to the ideas of ordered lives and full citizenship, themes which are taken up later.

At the same time, reaching a certain age, leaving school and receiving an independent income, however meagre, marked a qualitative difference in the relationship between parent and child and provided the basis for change in the power relationship between the generations.

The relationship between parent and child is, of course, negotiable from birth. Some young children 'get away with things', others are defined as 'spoilt' – implying that the child has made an inroad into parental authority. The period of late adolescence and early adulthood, from the mid-teens to, possibly, the early twenties, however, is characterized by a more intense negotiation than previously. At this transitional stage, boundaries between parental control and the young person's independence and freedom are redrawn and the limits of responsibility, rights and duties, on both sides, are explored in the attempt to transpose the relationship to one between adults. The success or otherwise of such familial renegotiation is indeed the substance of much drama and literature.

In a variety of ways, the scarcity of jobs for young people affected this changing balance of power and influenced the negotiations amongst family members. The discrepancies between the ascribed status of age and the achieved one of worker could be increased; thus just when young people were expecting a relaxation in parental control, such control could, in fact, be extended both within and beyond the confines of the family. This did not arise from pleasure in the exercise of parental power (although, perhaps, this should not be discounted) nor primarily because these parents felt that their unemployed children should be punished. It grew out of concern for them. Furthermore, status relationships between siblings were affected. This section looks at those benefits conferred by paid employment which assist the development of independence, and at some of the inhibiting effects of economic recession upon the ability of people (both employed and unemployed) to renegotiate their position within the family.

Independence is enhanced by several features of paid work: first, status is conferred by being the possessor of a job; second, status and power accrue from earned income; and, third, power flows from the entry into a new set of work and social relationships.

The mere fact of having paid employment accords status and prestige both within and outside the family. In the Newcastle study, to 'have a job' marked a person out as one of a highly regarded group, clearly expressed in Mrs Freeman's comment, 'Most of his friends couldn't get jobs. He was one of the elite.' To have paid work was important to the individual for the image conveyed and in the sense of identity it gave. Some (both old and young) displayed the insignia of their position. 'You say,' recounted Mr Freeman, '"Why didn't you stay and wash your hands?" . . . he has dirty hands, and he says he hasn't time, but he *has* time. I think he just likes to show he's been working' (emphasis in original).

In addition, the blossoming young workers were not only proud of themselves but were recipients of parental pride and, for some, shame was attached to the loss of a job:

I thought, 'Ee, he can't even keep his first job'. . . .I'd no more dream of telling anyone Martin had been given four-and-a-half months' notice. I didn't even tell Doris next door. Again because I felt . . . I felt ashamed. I was so proud of him getting a job when he first left school.

(Mrs Pearce)

Loss of a job was described in terms of being cashiered, an aspect of identity and selfhood forcibly and visibly removed. 'It strips them of their self respect. It definitely did my lassie,' said Mrs McGuinness of her daughter's eighteen-month unemployment following the closure of her firm. Kathleen McGuinness described herself to her mother as sacked, 'not being able to keep my first job', despite the loss arising from circumstances outside her control.

Having a job also influenced one's standing with other family members. Amongst brothers and sisters work bestowed status and privilege which overrode notions of equality and fairness. Parents felt constrained to legitimate this, whatever the heartache, because of the moral superiority attached to work and the worker. For example, in a dispute with her unemployed brother, a working daughter had first choice in the selection of television programmes:

She [her daughter] says, 'I've just come in from work,' and all that. 'You've got your telly upstairs', a black and white . . . and he wanted to watch snooker. Well what can you do, I mean, she's going out to work. . . .So he just gives in . . . reluctantly like.

(Mrs Clark)

More subtly, however, by obtaining a job at a time recognized as the 'correct' time in the individual's life course, a young person assumes the appropriate status in the age hierarchy of sibling relationships.[10] Disjunction between age and employment status was apparent in the ribbing amongst siblings as employment statuses fluctuated, individuals becoming the recipients of jokes and comments according to whether they were in or out of work. The Drake brothers, for example, each in turn referred to the other as 'dole wallah' as each moved in and out of temporary work. This did not mean that brothers and sisters were not supportive of each other or caring. There was substantial evidence that they were. But dependency, lack of status and the ensuing lack of authority, all components of unemployment, were not only keenly felt but were brought to the attention of the individual concerned in ways ranging from the absolute lack of funds to the minor irritations and humiliations of family life.

Status was particularly marked over the recurrent and fraught issue of 'staying in bed' and getting up late when unemployed. It was in sharp contrast to the right of employed people to 'lie in' at weekends or on their day off. The complexity of this behaviour is explored in the next chapter.

A vital element in independence is, of course, money; and all the young people in this study had income of some kind – whether from wages or from state benefits. However, as Lewis has noted, 'Denied the traditional route to independence many young people are forced back onto the secondary method of income distribution – the social security system' (Lewis 1985: 4).

The social security system, however, is secondary in more than one sense. As noted earlier, importance was attached to the way in which money was acquired; the fact that it was earned rather than merely received or donated was seen by many respondents to confer status and self-respect. The 'dole' was frequently portrayed not only as degrading but as less deserved. Thus while the pitiable amounts left from unemployment benefit were in the control of a young person when family commitments had been satisfied, a similarly small sum of earned money in a 'proper' job was invested with a different meaning. In the instance cited in the last chapter, when discussing with his mother the offer of a cleaning job to Kathleen McGuinness, her brother observed: 'At least she'll think, "Well I've worked for it, I haven't just signed my name"'.[11]

This period in a person's life was seen as a stage when, as one mother put it, they should 'have money in their pockets'. The amount of money a young person has at his or her disposal is, of course, important for the exploration of the new freedoms open to them: to spend on personal necessities and pleasures, to go out with and meet friends. Young people in the study commented on the social restrictions and petty economies which low income imposed. Money, however, is important in more subtle ways to the texture of affective relationships. Income allows the individual to be generous. In this respect, while those on low wages were often at a disadvantage, those relying upon state benefits inevitably were. Keith Hills described how his older brother sometimes paid for him. 'He'll say, "Coming out tonight? Fancy a pint?" and I'll say, "I've got no money," and he'll say, "Never mind."' And Mr Clark spoke of the situation between his three children. His 21-year-old daughter helped her 19-year-old unemployed brother to buy a computer (his consuming interest) by putting down the deposit. 'She helps them all the way,' he said. (The brother and sister referred to here were, incidentally, the two who had competed for precedence over the colour television.) He also described his younger, 17-year-old son's reaction to getting a job:

> He's got his own job now, he gets his own money now. He thinks he's all great now, with his own money now. He goes round wanting to buy his mother everything now. It makes all the difference . . . once they get a job it makes them happy. He was just sitting there down in the dumps, day after day.

The matter is not trivial; gifts are an important component of social relationships, as recipients of charity are well aware. Thus, while brothers, sisters and parents were frequently generous with the young unemployed and lent, gave or paid for an outing from affection, nonetheless, giving confers power upon the giver. As Mauss (1954) observed, and to which Leonard (1980) drew attention in her description of how mothers keep their children close to them, 'If people accept your gifts you own part of their soul; they return your affection and allow you to have some say in their lives' (Mauss 1954, cited by Leonard 1980:63).

The flowering independence drew sustenance not only from a job and income, but also from the new network of relationships ensuing from employment. From these, young people could build up their own cultural and social capital. There were both personal and societal overtones. One father in particular saw the workplace as the only site where full maturity could develop: 'The only way to learn to be an adult is to be with adults. Unless you have the chance to work . . . where else are you going to do it?' In his view, his son's maturity waxed and waned according to whether he was in or out of work. Whether the boy was responding to the expectations of the different milieux in which he found himself, or whether the change lay in his father's perceptions of him, is difficult to judge. Nonetheless, this father was making a point which not only has implications for personal development but also for the wider society.

Carmichael recently wrote of 'young unemployed people who did not know anyone older than themselves, other than their parents; of unemployed young people living in separate strata –

16s-18s, 19–20s – with no adults around, as you get in a workshop or an office' (Carmichael 1986: 233). Such adults are not only able to offer advice but they are also the means by which young people learn informally – for example, through overheard conversations – about how someone solved problems at work or at home. On the personal and wider cultural effects, she continues:

> How do you learn about your identity as a worker if you don't have an employer? How do you learn about fair wages if you never had a wage packet? Where do you get a sense of your own political strength if you have no industrial arena in which to test it out?
>
> (Carmichael 1986: 233)

The points she makes echo and expand the understanding of rights and citizenship sensed by parents who intervened with employers over the treatment of their children and were outraged at the low wages and exploitative conditions which some of them suffered.

As well as advancing such maturity, the fresh associations young people made at work, not just with older people but also with those of their own age, provided a source of new power, the power to resist parental control. Such associations, moreover, lay beyond the control of parents in a way that the earlier ones of school and neighbourhood had not. New friends from work gave a young person leverage in the negotiations with parents over the extension of independence. This leverage forced parents to recognize that the boundaries of control could be, and were being, pushed back. Kathleen McGuinness drew obvious courage from her new contacts: 'As I say, I tend . . . now to stop at Suzanne's overnight even though I know Mam doesn't like it. She [mother] said it was my decision, so I did. . . .'

There was also, however, a delicacy, sensitivity and regard for parents in such testing of boundaries. The same girl described another occasion when she said to her new friend,

> 'No, I'm going straight home.' She says, 'What's the matter?' ('cos I normally go in for a cup of coffee). I says, 'Oh . . .', 'Cos me mam had said, you know, 'Are you going to be out late?' [mimics]. So I says to her, 'I'm going straight home to keep mummy's face happy.'

For the unemployed young person, however, the shift in the balance of power could be the opposite of that which they had expected on leaving school. Parental concern that their children obtain work could perpetuate the older established relationship between parent and child, one of more overt prescriptions and pressures. Such actions, it should be emphasized, did not arise because of the contribution any earnings would make to the household finances (although in some cases a child's contribution was vital to the household economy), nor solely from the feeling that the child should now be self-sufficient. It stemmed, rather, from an awareness that waged work was essential to the future well-being of the child, and it was accompanied by a concern which some expressed about the erosion of any positive attitudes towards work which the young had already developed.

The overtones were both economic and moral. As Mrs Robson explained:

> It's easy for people to get into a rut if you *start* off your life not knowing what work is but you're still going to get kept. Maybe it's a minimum, but you're still getting kept, aren't you? It might be easy to go that way (emphasis in original).

The ensuing pressure on children to search for jobs, and the strategies adopted to defray the effects of an unstructured day, must have seemed like a continuation or even an intensification of strategies parents employ with much younger children – for example, the nagging and joking, the insistence, by some, on not staying in bed late, and, in some cases, the threats.

By definition many of the issues would not have arisen had the young person been in work, and the social and economic power conferred by work would have rendered any conflict over behaviour more negotiable or even allowed it to be viewed with tolerance and indulgence; parents would feel more obliged to modify their demands, and young people would be bolder in making exploratory forays to extend the bounds of their self-determination and independence.

The response of the unemployed young ranged from frustration, annoyance and retreat – some up to their bedrooms, others leaving home. One girl, for example, now living with her married sister prior to moving into her own flat, had left home for such reasons. There were few cases of young people leaving home in this study, but friends and acquaintances had left over the issue of joblessness because of the tensions this created. The absence of the constraints upon behaviour imposed by employment and the mere physical presence of the unemployed person in the home during working hours was conducive to irritation, if not tension. Some young people, however, managed to occupy their days in ways acceptable to other members of the family but in so doing limited their own sense of independence and individualism. Some, for example, took over the domestic responsibility for the home, others quietly did the tasks other members of the family neglected or forgot to do.

As noted elsewhere (Allatt and Yeandle 1986), parents in this situation tread a tightrope between compulsion and protectiveness, and in some cases the uneasy tensions between these two aspects of parenting were brought into sharp focus. When Phil Matthews left school abruptly at 17, 'naturally we were disappointed,' said his mother, 'and Dad said, "Right, no work, no home, *out*."' 'He got his marching orders,' said Mr Matthews. Paternal authority was used, here, to effect (Phil obtained unskilled work the next day), but Mrs Matthews' role in averting further conflict over the issue was also evident. She felt 'very sympathetic' towards her son, and stressed that 'I didn't want him and his Dad to break over it.'

There is, however, a further dimension to consider: familial power in the public domain. The impact of recession on the power relationships between the generations was not confined to families where the young person was unemployed. Although many of the young people in the study wished to obtain work through their own efforts, some had been forced by the paucity of available work to accept a parent's offer to 'speak for them'. When this happens, some measure of responsibility for good performance in the job falls on the parent; it signals an implicit contract with the employer (Jenkins *et al.* 1983). By extension, parental supervision over the young person is increased and obligation to the parent on the part of the child is extended. The following comments made by Mrs Hamilton about her son illustrate this:

> Well, we've had no trouble with him . . . from when he started the job because I mean . . . apart from anything else he doesn't want to let his dad down. . . . After all, his dad got him the job and . . . he was told that before he started. . . . Me and my husband said, 'Now whatever you do, don't let me down. You've been lucky enough – very lucky – to get the job . . . stick at it.' You know how you do – you talk to them. 'Oh, yes, Dad, I know.'

Thus, at a time when a young person is expecting a slackening of parental control, parental authority, now endowed through the chain of commitment to a parent who has received a favour from an employer, is imported from the private domain of the family into the public domain of the workplace. This father was particularly conscious of the dilemma between the need for a job, which meant submitting to parental constraints at work, and the fragile developing independence of his son. He tried to mitigate the situation by encouraging his son to leave for work before he himself left. The strategy, however, reflects the contradictions which recession creates:

> I cycle to work . . . and Peter, he'll either walk or get the bus, so about 7 o'clock I'll say to Peter, 'Right, you skidaddle off, an' I'll see you at work.' An' I leave about ten past, yer know. . . .[I] suppose I could go to work *with* 'im, walk *with* him, but as I say, I want him to be a little bit independent, yer know what I mean. I don't want him to keep relyin' on his dad *too* much (emphasis in original).

CONCLUSION

It is true that today paid employment, especially that of men, largely takes place outside the home. This has the consequence that few children are familiar with the details of adult work. Emphasizing this divorce between the public domain of paid employment and the private domain of family life conceals, however, not only the interdependence of the domains but also the continuing role of the family in the construction of economic identities[12] and independence.

From an early age, within the family children are orientated to the world of work. It is an orientation which is embedded in the language of daily life, in family routines and in family practices. Ideas about work and the pervasiveness of the work ethic, whether people conform to this or not, were apparent amongst the Newcastle families in how they dealt with the economics of family life, in the economic values parents encouraged in their children and in the nurturing of proper attitudes and habits. It pervaded attitudes to time, timekeeping and the moral imperatives surrounding work and work identities and was sustained by the idea of work as paid employment. Amongst the families studied, paid employment and the associated income were seen as underpinning the ability to survive, as well as underpinning independence and the progression through the stages of the life course which people considered to be normal, culminating in marriage and settling down.

Whilst recognizing the sway of the material advantages of an income from a proper job, when ideas about work have such deep familial roots and have from early infancy been structured into one's sense of self, it is perhaps not surprising that unemployed young people continue to want work even when the labour market holds out little promise, and that the work ethic retains its grip.[13]

It is within this complex of economic and moral values and the practices they underpin that young people negotiate within the family for increased independence. It is at a stage in the life course which is heralded by leaving school and entering the labour market. During this period of transition, the processes out of which independence is built and strengthened through interaction amongst family members are thrown into disarray by a depressed labour market.

Paid employment confers cultural, economic and social power which can be used to renegotiate one's place in the configuration of family relationships – that is, with parents and siblings. Thus the status of worker, the power of money, the social capital of new friendships at work – in the public domain beyond the control of parents – all provide resources which can be used to push back the boundaries of parental control. Economic recession, however, interrupts the anticipated and expected progression to independence for both unemployed and employed. The unemployed find they are accorded a low status about which many feel a sense of shame, they have little economic power, little money to spend, lend or buy gifts, and what they receive in state benefits frequently does not carry the same moral worth as money that is earned. They are deprived of those work relationships which teach them about work identities, work itself and political power. Their position in the family seems to retreat to that of the increased dependency of childhood rather than the increased status they expected to achieve at this stage, and they may lose what they see as their proper place in the sibling hierarchy. For those in work but who have had to accept a parent's offer of help to obtain it, the parent's obligation to the employer and the young person's additional obligation to the parent extend parental power into the public domain of work, a place formerly associated with new freedoms. Finally, unemployment inhibits the assumption of full citizenship.

These breaks and distortions in the life course, in what is seen as the normal ordered progression, have largely focused upon the economic. The next chapter broadens the theme of disruption by looking at how economic recession undermines a sense of social order.

4

DISORDER IN TIME AND PLACE

INTRODUCTION: THE DIMENSIONS OF ORDER

The last chapter showed how a poor and deteriorating local labour market affected young people's transition to adulthood and independence in the context of family relationships. The expectations surrounding this transitional period, however, are aspects of a more general system of order by which people regulate and make sense of their lives. This chapter looks at other elements of this sense of order to illustrate how deeply economic and technological change can penetrate the private domain of the personal and domestic, producing disorder in the relationships of young people and their families.

It is not only in times of widely recognized social change that people are assailed by uncertainty. Society is always changing and, irrespective of historical change, change is inherent in the personal process of ageing and in the life events and transitions of life. There is, however, a paradox in how we experience change. In discussing the metaphors through which people define and shape their lives, Salmon (1985) draws attention to the paradox between reality which is constantly changing and the sense of stability we manage to impose upon our lives and which is accompanied by the notion of normal adult life as a period of settling down. This contradiction implies that somehow we construct for ourselves, out of the resources we have to hand, a sense of order and predictability, and it follows that this social order we create is fragile and vulnerable.

Social order, therefore, is not just a problem for sociologists and social theory; it is also a problem for people in their everyday lives, and severe changes in society disturb the expectations and practices out of which some order has been carved. As the last chapter showed, a changing society can disrupt both the expected pattern of life course transitions which people define as normal and the interweaving of the life course strands of several careers such as those referred to by Brannen (1987): employment careers, domestic careers, household careers and consumption careers. Unemployment disrupts what Zerubavel (1981) refers to as career timetables.

Social order can, of course, be harsh as well as benign. In the present case the benign form is assumed. In its ideal form social order for the individual connotes a sense of well-being: physical, psychological and social; of being at one with oneself and the world. It encompasses a sense of control and direction, of the ability to organize one's life and plan ahead, as well as a sense of appropriateness, of there being a right time, a right place and a correct sequence in which things are done. It includes a sense of fit, of belonging and being part of things. It assumes a certain predictability in behaviour and responses – one's own and those of others – and a broad predictability of events.

Social order is constructed out of the resources which are available and is embedded in social relationships. For example, access to and use of such resources as income, work, time, space and affection take place in competition with, co-operation with or synchronization with others, and meanings and moralities are attached to these resources and their deployment. Thus social order is not merely an attribute of personality, of being organized, enabling a person to impose his or her stamp upon the environment, although individual psychological differences should not be discounted; people do vary in their ability to utilize resources.

In the construction of social order, resources are intricately interwoven. Health and well-being, work in paid employment, time, space and the emotional capital of affection and satisfactory relationships were salient here.[1] The loss of, or inability to obtain, paid employment and the attached status of a highly regarded income, however, were the dominating resources which reverberated upon the others, setting in motion complex interactions.

Health and well-being, for example, and family harmony were the most apparent casualties of the loss of a place in the labour market. These were not only due to the loss of status and income of paid employment but were also grounded in the repercussions of a person's unemployment upon domestic time and space.

THE SEARCH FOR ORDER

That people strive to impose predictability and continuity upon their lives was clear from the way in which the young people and their parents described their daily lives and how they saw their future. As Salmon (1985) observed, the many forms this took were distilled in the widespread sentiments of being settled and secure, referring, amongst these families, particularly to jobs and ultimately marriage.

Because of the experiences in the labour market, described in the earlier chapters, it is not surprising that being 'settled in a job', meaning a 'proper' job with pay that was considered 'appropriate' and 'fair', was a recurrent theme. The idea of fairness coloured many comments and is discussed in the next chapter. These young adults were, moreover, on the brink of the next stage in the process of 'settling down' – courtship and marriage or some permanent relationship, steps intimately related to prior establishment in the labour market. This kind of future, generally considered to be normal in our culture, is epitomized in the following comments by Philip Thompson and Neil Peters, respectively: 'Everybody wants something to live on – just a roof over their head, a decent wage . . . and sort of like a little bit of money in their pocket to spend.'

> I don't *seriously* think about a few years time. . . .I just sit and say, 'Well, I *hope* I'll be like this . . . and I hope in five years time we'll be married,[2] settled down, and I hope to be doing a career, whatever I'm doing . . . to have a nice house,' just the normal things which everybody wishes, you know (emphasis in original).

Being 'settled' was also seen as a mental state of well-being, linked to a sense of security and contentment. As Mrs Jones observed, relating individual well-being to society in general, 'A person's got to be happy in their job. . . .I think it makes for a better world. . . .If you're happy in your work . . . but if you're unsettled, y'know. . . .' And the metaphor used by Neil Peters, brought up in the care of the local authority, encapsulates the contrast between change and a deep-seated longing for consistency and security, felt perhaps more keenly by him but present for many of us:

I want a settled life for once, because all my life I've been shifted about. . . .I've lost and gained friendships all the time. I just want to get some friendships and keep them, have people who I love around us, and I just want to keep them there, sort of in a little nutshell.

Whilst 'being settled' was the ultimate aim, people's responses also conveyed the sense that there should be an orderliness to life in general. Some responses were rooted in particular conceptualizations of time and were shaped by metaphor. A perception of time as linear was associated with a view of the life course as a journey, time marked by specific events occurring at specific stages, at the 'proper' time in one's progression – some routes, however, leading to 'nowhere' or 'dead ends'. This sometimes gave way to a view of life as a flowing current along which the individual was carried, still linear but providing metaphors of interrupted flow, of eddies and backwaters. Another pattern was that of cyclical time present in the recurring schedule of the daily routine (Zerubavel 1981). These ways of seeing and experiencing time were not mutually exclusive but intimately linked.

The metaphor of life as a journey, broadly mapped out, was particularly prominent. As these families had been selected because at least one member was in that transitional period between the dependency of childhood and the independence of full adulthood and 'being settled', symbolically marked in our society by marriage, the emphasis upon those life career events clustered in this period and immediately beyond was not unexpected. Leaving school, a job, a period of youthful enjoyment, courtship, marriage, a home of one's own and the establishment of an independent family unit were seen as being ordered in a specific sequence; as Mrs Hills pointed out, 'then she started work, then she started courting, everything seemed, y'know, clear'. This is not to say that all adhere to this sequence, but this order was broadly felt to be proper even by those who might appear to lack foresight or by those with little opportunity to obtain work. Thus the relationship of this cash nexus between employment and domestic career was even evident in Philip Thompson's comment, 'When I decide to get married, then I'll get a job.'

This notion of ordered progression also appeared in comments on the nature and sequencing of jobs themselves, although a poor labour market could modify this by lowering aspirations. Again it was bound up with the idea of security. You needed security so that you could look forward to things, have prospects – for example, 'full money' following an apprenticeship. 'Prospects have to be at the end of anything,' said Martin Johnson, 'or it isn't any good.' Even lowly jobs, it was felt, should contain an element of training, and as described in the earlier chapters, the absence of training accounted for the dissatisfaction young people and parents felt about some jobs and some government schemes for young people. You should, said one young woman, be able 'to build up, pick things up as you go along'. As the quotation below suggests, this sense of progression and consolidation is epitomized for working-class males in the North-East by apprenticeship in a skilled trade which, as noted in earlier chapters, continues to rank highly in people's aspirations despite the decline in such opportunities and the erosion of their industrial base:

> Interviewer: How do you see things for your sons in, say, five years' time?
> Mrs Rice: Well, I hope they're both in their trade . . . and got good jobs. I would like to see them established in a good job because, in four or five years' time . . . Martin'll be what, going on for 27, Gerald will be 24, you know. . . .I hope they've got themselves well established by then.

Progression for girls may be differently perceived. If, as Salmon (1985) suggests, a girl's journey reaches an unmapped plateau after marriage, in contrast to a male's path which continues to be signposted, it may account for the emphasis by some (not all) on the greater importance of work for boys during these early years in the labour market because, as one mother observed, 'That's been the role of a boy. . . . That's what they function for . . . they leave school, they get a job, they get married, they look after a family. I mean that's their whole purpose in life.' It is worth noting that because of this Mr Harris felt that unemployment would affect the health 'of the lads more than it would girls'.

The idiom in which the responses were couched suggested that this journey was not without its hazards even in times when the sequencing of these junctures in the life course was not threatened. It was a pathway from which one could stray or be deflected. At each crossroad, when making decisions about leaving school or entering jobs or marriage, young people had to be careful to 'take the right step'. Good parenting included 'putting them on the right foot' or giving 'them a start' like the father who paid the first instalment of a savings account. The role of parents, as Shirley Hewitt observed, was 'to keep you on the right track', explained by her mother as seeing that her daughter was 'keeping the right hours, and things like that'. This is discussed later with the notion of the good citizen.

The last two quotations hint at the relationship between the lifelong journey and the daily routines of family life, between individual time and domestic time. Order was embedded in cyclical/diurnal as well as linear time, for daily activities were seen as profoundly affecting the quality and appropriateness of the 'luggage' taken on the lifelong journey. This view was particularly evident in comments on timekeeping and the associated traits of reliability and responsibility referred to in the last chapter: of children never having to be pestered to get up in the morning, parents and children being good timekeepers, never being late for work, never having a day off work even when feeling ill. The importance lay in the fact that such characteristics were the outward signs of a good worker, a reputation for which might secure a job, thereby setting and keeping oneself on the appropriate track for life's journey.

The underlying order and organization of the recurring days and how this entered personal dispositions was revealed in the diaries informants were asked to keep for one day. 'Being organized' was a characteristic of this order, extending from personal tidiness to planning one's life. Comments on 'keeping their bedroom tidy', or their personal space within it, frequently formed the first response to questions about young people and household tasks. Some were so obsessed by tidiness that it became a self-deprecating joke: Mr Hills said his family referred to him as the 'top man' because he systematically replaced the toothpaste and shampoo tops irritatingly left off by other members of his family. Furthermore, organization was not the sole prerogative of those in work, as Mrs Kelly, mother in a family where all were unemployed, commented: 'You've got to organize yourself when you're on the dole, because if you don't, you'll be borrowing and ticking and worrying yourself stiff. . . .It's the only way I can manage.' Her son also described the disciplined and rigid timekeeping she insisted upon for meals.

The motif of well-being and being at ease underlay pursuits for orderliness. It appeared in Mr Freeman's reason for building an extension to the house: 'then they can all use this . . . working area. . . .There's washing every other day, y'know . . . I don't like it. I cannot say I'm in comfort . . . when I see washing lying around. . . .I cannot really relax.'

Unemployment, which all except seven young people had experienced, profoundly affected this search for order and sense of predictability to life. The clearest indicators of disorder were the effects upon physical and mental health and the changed and fluctuating atmosphere of the home.

It should be said that work in itself is not necessarily conducive to health and well-being. Even in this small study, for example, one mother felt that her son's health was impaired by the nature of his (well-paid) occupation; and in a restructuring labour market some young people and their parents felt that working conditions were deteriorating. In contrast, Geoffrey Lewis, whilst disliking his unemployed state and feeling a sense of estrangement from his family, nonetheless felt that his health had improved due to his increased involvement in physical activities. There is also debate on the relative effects upon health and unemployment and the accompanying drop in income (Carr-Hill 1987).[3] The prevalence of parental subsidies for this age group, however, must at least cushion the nutritional effects of reduced income.

To have paid work, however, as earlier chapters have shown, was deemed important. The uncertain labour market created anxieties, and many people were conscious of changes in physical and psychological well-being which seemed to flow from unemployment and appeared to fluctuate according to whether or not the young person was in work. Latent long-standing complaints, such as psoriasis and asthma, could erupt; several reported symptoms listed in Fagin and Little's (1984) Malaise Inventory include moodiness, worry and irritability. Many said they had been, or were, or would very likely be, depressed. 'Not that I'd hang myself, or anything like that,' added Martin Pearce. It was an ambiguous, interstitial state between health and sickness. '[Unemployment] gets you bad-tempered,' said Carol Knight, in phrases replete with metaphor:

> It really wears you out. I've got a bottle there off the doctor, for depr- . . . well not really depression, but just to keep us going . . . but I only take it when I feel run down. . . .[H]e said I just needed a pick-me-up.

Increased levels of depression following prolonged unemployment have been found in other studies of young people (e.g. Banks and Jackson 1982), and there is a greater likelihood of the young unemployed being depressed, anxious and generally in a poor emotional state than the young employed (*New Society* 1985).

Parents, however, not only described the changes in their children as they gained or lost jobs, but described their children as changed people. Mr Hamilton 'watched the change' in his son: 'he became . . . morbid, miserable, hard to communicate with, bad-tempered'. When his son eventually obtained work, his father commented, 'I think he feels more a member of the family again. . . .He's starting to function more in the house. Oh, he's a changed lad, definitely.'

The disorder was not confined to the anxiety, moodiness and lack of well-being in the young person but, in a variety of ways, penetrated the lives of other family members and drew upon the reserves of emotional capital of love and affection they might have. The moodiness, irritability and increased sensitivity and withdrawal of the young person could, for example, raise a mixture of shared misery, empathy, sympathy, irritation, support and worry amongst parents and siblings. Some of the underlying intricacies in the shaping of such responses which were based in conceptions and use of time and space are discussed later in the chapter. Here Mrs McGuinness' description of the effect of her daughter's unemployment upon her family gives some idea of the unpredictability and disorientation which the situation created. She was full of praise for the way her older employed sons and their wives had supported Kathleen, taking her away for weekends, out in the evenings, and giving her driving lessons, but she also recounted how even in a caring family a child's response to unemployment could irritate:

> Oh, her dad, he said, 'She's getting on my nerves sitting around.' So I says, 'Well, what can you do?' I says, 'You can't bray her out [beat it out of her].' The boys have been a good help, but it's hell to see a kid going on like that.

Unemployment could also inhibit the usual pattern of communication between people; in extreme cases it could break down altogether. In this case Mrs McGuinness acted as the intermediary, interpreter and conciliator:

> I really think her brothers felt for her because they used to come in the back to me and say, 'Has she been out today?' I'd say, 'No luck, no.' But she got so moody

they just stopped asking *her*. . . .I think she took it as jibing, and I used to say, 'They're not, they're concerned about you.' 'Why do they go on about it?' (emphasis in original).

Thresholds of tolerance for other aspects of family intercourse were lowered by the misery of unemployment. Rejection of horseplay and teasing, part of the intimate discourse of family life, could eventually evoke petulance and a feeling that sharp steps should be taken to bring a sibling back into line, as Mrs McGuinness recounted:

There used to be tears, and their wives used to say to them, 'Leave her alone.' And of course Malcolm says, 'Oh, she's petty.' He says, 'You know what it is, mam, she wants a good slap.' And, of course, when she used to cry I used to go in the other room and I used to have a cry too.

Discord could also arise from different perceptions of the situation. As noted earlier, some employed parents, even those who had been unemployed themselves, felt that jobs were there for those willing to work, and their children felt misunderstood. Angela Ward described her father's response to her unemployed state: 'He just says, "She should gan an' get herself a job," and things like that. But I do, I'm always at the job centre. He thinks it's easy.'

Because of the way in which the informants were reached, there was only one instance of anyone leaving home because of these stresses, although some recounted how friends had left home. And the support which parents tried to give could carry costs not only for the relationships between parent and child but also between husband and wife. Jokes can go too far, and there is a fine borderline between persistent pressure and nagging. Mrs Robson eventually 'blew up' at her husband:

He used to be on their *backs* and that and . . . well, it does get unpleasant. Nagging doesn't get you anywhere and he nags. You know, we have more rows than enough about him nagging, and he *tries* to stop but he cannot. He just nags *on* and *on* and *on*. I just sometimes let it go in one ear and out the other, then I cannot stand it any more so I blow up with him (emphasis in original).

Mrs Matthews, referred to earlier, who did not want her husband and son 'to break' over the matter of his getting employment when he suddenly left school against their wishes, obviously mediated a similar situation.

OUT OF TIME, OUT OF PLACE

At a deeper level than these manifestations of disorder in personal well-being and family relations, and indeed contributing to them, were disorientations of time and place. In his book, *Hidden Rhythms*, Zerubavel (1981) analyses the schedules and calendars of social life and notes how temporal regularity in our social world enhances our cognitive well-being. Unemployment, anxieties about getting or retaining a job, uncertainties surrounding the shifting or more ruthless expression of norms governing relationships between employer and employed in a market where labour was abundant – all threatened the pursuit of order and predictability. This disruption of temporal regularity took several forms: it affected the life career, the daily schedule and participation in collective time.

According to Parkes,

> We all need to discover our sense of fit. . . .[W]e need the sense of being 'on course', a trajectory on the basis of which we can anticipate, plan and hope. . . .[A] sense of meaning in life can only arise out of a reasonable expectation that plans will be fulfilled.
>
> (Parkes 1984: 14)

Plans, however, could come to nought. For example, encouraging children to pursue higher education as described in Chapter Two – that is, following the societal tenets acclaimed as good parenting – did not guarantee the expected outcome of a good job. As Mrs Hills commented:

> there isn't any . . . *real* . . . future for them anyway, you don't know what's ahead for them. . . .I mean, I always had great plans for mine when. . . .Everybody dreams what their kids are gonna be. I mean . . . as far as I'm concerned, Keith's done everything that anybody could want to have. . . .I mean the others have been marvellous but . . . Keith went to university, got a degree an' everything . . . but he hasn't worked for 18 months.

94

The effect of the devaluation of their advice left parents with a sense of guilt. Persuading children to stay on at school an additional year in an attempt to increase their children's own resources need offer no advantage whatsoever. 'You feel that you've wasted their time,' said Mrs Robson. The signals about the rewards of education did not coincide with experience. This apparent devaluation of the resource of education must have induced a feeling that the resource of parental advice was also of less value, less 'tuned in' to the times. Chances of employment or job training could also be reduced as young people passed certain age barriers; even limited aspirations had to be lowered. As discussed earlier, in Chapter Two, it was felt to be a matter of your 'face fitting', who you knew rather than what you knew, and that 'qualifications' do not get you anywhere these days.

Moreover, an apparently ordered life could suddenly be disrupted. Good starts could become dead ends as the labour market contracted and restructured. The effect upon individual well-being is clear in Mr Phillip's account of his own and his son's reactions to the sudden redundancy which ruptured the sequencing of life course events and the interweaving of domestic, employment and consumption careers:

> You feel sick, I mean you say, 'Oh hell. Well what the hell is he going to do now? He's just 20-year-old and where'll he get a job?' You just feel a bit sick. Plus, I mean, he's got his car now, he's courting strong and all of a sudden he goes from getting on and enjoying himself, buying himself a car, to *nothing* and it's a big, big drop. He's been bad-tempered and moody since he got finished and that's just in a month (emphasis in original).

Whilst older workers referred to themselves and their lives as being finished, younger people could not rely on even starting theirs. There were such comments as being 'too old at 17', 'retired at 18', being 'back to square one'. Expected and anticipated journeys turned into unpredictable games of snakes and ladders.

Nor could the expected patterning of young lives be followed. Lack of money affected both the character and quality of life. 'He doesn't go out, with not having any money. And that's what I don't like. I mean, he should be out, enjoying himself at his age, and he's *not*' (emphasis in original) (Mr Hamilton). It meant that they could not afford, unless subsidized, the current trends in clothes worn by other members of their age group. Mrs Hills neatly summarized the effect: 'It makes them feel even *more* out of it. They're out of it as it is – when they can't get work – without being out of fashion as well' (emphasis in original). Moreover, those critical staging posts of this part of the journey, culminating in the setting up of an independent household, were threatened. As Mrs Hills observed:

> I wouldn't encourage them to get married or anything while they're unemployed because I don't think it's fair . . . that . . . to be gettin' married and get involved with anyone. . . .I wouldn't like to think of them gettin' married while they were on the social security and then . . . starting a family.[4]

Her unemployed son felt excluded from the mainstream of life as he watched the courting and engagements of his employed friends.

But, as this mother recognized, there are routes to independence other than obtaining a job in the local labour market. Some are quite legitimate, some combined legitimacy with moral disapproval, some are illegal. Of whatever cast, all that were raised here were frequently accompanied by a sense of disquiet. These alternative ways to an income were working away from the parental home, crime, fiddle jobs (drawing state benefit whilst in paid employment) and dependence upon state benefit.

As an earlier quotation illustrated, for young people to leave home in order to find paid employment could produce an emotional wrench; it did not seem right to be forced to move in order to have work, although leaving home to get married was another matter. Because of the method of selecting the families, none of the young people had themselves left home to seek work, although some had considered it and a few had older brothers and sisters now in their mid-twenties who had taken the step, usually following redundancy or job insecurity and unemployment. The jobs included engineering contract work in the South Atlantic, waitressing and hotel work in the South, and nannying both in this country and abroad. Others had older brothers who had in the past worked in London or on oil rigs in the North Sea but who were currently back in the North-East and unemployed, and one girl had a brother who had joined the Army at 18.

Whilst parents had accepted these decisions to move away from home, they were anxious as to how their children would fare in a strange environment where they might be taken advantage of or worse. Mrs Jenkins described how Anne was never off the phone at first. 'I'm homesick, I'm coming home.' I worried how she would get on because I knew how soft she was. People sort of take a lend [take advantage] of her. But she proved she can manage.

And Mr Hamilton explained why he had never really encouraged his son to leave home in search of work:

you know, the influx of violence in society now, and things like that. And being on his own, and at the finish I wasn't too happy with the idea meself. To be quite honest, I – I never encouraged him, other than to join the forces, to ever leave home.

In regions with a history of high unemployment such as the North-East, the Armed Forces have been a traditional destination for young men. It was ironic, however, that if jobs had to be sought away from home, recruitment into the forces, given their *raison d'être*, gave parents greater peace of mind than distant civilian jobs, especially if young people were considering leaving home in order to search for a job rather than going to a specific appointment.

Mrs Kelly illuminates Mr Hamilton's comment above. The Army, it seemed, was seen as a surrogate family in that it provided a structure of order and control:

I'd sooner have me kids on the dole rather than look for a job away from home. If he wanted to go in the Army, fair enough. I'd know where they were; but as for going away for jobs, I'd be worried what they were up to, where they were living, what they were living on.

THE MORAL ORDER

Unemployment is thus seen as a threat to the moral order. Young people could be drawn into bad ways. As noted in the last chapter and at the beginning of this one, parenting included putting and trying to keep children on the right road. It was seen in the attempt to convey the balance between the freedom of independence and the limits imposed by what is generally recognized as reasonable and responsible behaviour. Such behaviour ranged from consideration for others, being sensible and reliable, to keeping within the bounds of the law. These behaviours were elements of good citizenship.

In family behaviour these elements found voice, for example, in attempts to persuade a son to lower the volume of a record player: 'I can't get him to be reasonable,' complained Mrs Hamilton. 'I've no reason to complain,' said another mother, '. . . she's very considerate of the neighbours.' Many parents kept a critical eye on friendships and 'keeping the right hours'. Not bringing trouble to the door was frequently used as a commendation of their children. Being 'reasonable' and 'taking everything in moderation' summed up the general approach parents hoped to inculcate.

Unemployment, however, posed dilemmas. People were surrounded by anomalies, illogicalities and injustices. There was also a lot of spare time in which to 'get up to things'. There were ways of obtaining money which fell well outside the legitimate journey that parents had hoped for and, in hard times, while parents had put their children on the right path there could be greater temptations to stray from it than in 'normal' circumstances.

Thus, while parents felt that young people should have 'money in their pockets at their age', there were ways of getting money which were not approved of. Peter Hamilton, now employed but who had been 'sick of being on the dole' after sixteen months, said he would 'do anything to get money – well, not kill'. Most references, however, were to theft and burglary. The popular, though unproven, notion that unemployment gave rise to increased burglary was voiced by several respondents. One mother could not accept this reasoning. Crime had not, she argued, increased in the '30s when unemployment was also high. Another, however, suggested a sense of injustice as a possible explanation of the property crime imputed to unemployed young people:

> I think, probably, they've got a grudge against society because they think like, well . . . 'What's the matter with us? Why can't *we* work?' [B]ecause, I mean, they're bound to know that their parents at one time have worked . . . and probably older brothers and sisters have worked. And they'll be looking at themselves . . . and saying 'Why am I so different?' (emphasis in original)

Thus, while income from such a source was defined as illegitimate, some parents feared that crime might become increasingly tempting to young people if unemployment showed no signs of remission.

Dilemmas surrounded the idea of fiddle money – from jobs on

the side when drawing state benefit. Mrs Robson, fearing a slide into attitudes and behaviour of which she disapproved, firmly said she would not allow her son to do fiddle jobs; she would put her foot down: 'If you *let* them at *their* age and they get a taste of it, drawing *dole* money and fiddle, they will *not* want proper work' (emphasis in original). Others, however, were more ambivalent in their views. Fear of detection and a feeling that they, personally, would be unlucky enough to be caught should they take on fiddle jobs were great deterrents.

But while such statements were frequently accompanied by a sense of morality, about keeping within the bounds of the law, and of social order, this was sometimes modified by a sense of injustice and the sheer illogicality of regulations which discouraged people from taking on low-paid and often irregular work to supplement inadequate social security payments. Moreover, because so many were now unemployed, some sensed a relaxation in the moral pressure which formerly might inhibit those tempted to supplement their income in this way.

However, whilst entering the Armed Forces was deemed legitimate and respectable, though disruptive, the legitimate means of income from state benefit was not always approved of. To be reliant on the state for income was frequently deemed inappropriate for either the young person at home or as a basis for future independence. Such attitudes were not solely due to the smallness of such income, the indignities with which it could be surrounded and the quality of life it implied. The attitudes also drew upon the morality associated with money as a reward for work and the morality of work itself.

The ultimate dilemma was that of marriage and all that it stands for in our society: a cultural symbol representing independence, maturity and responsibility in a crystallized and idealized form. To be married connotes full citizenship in that societal responsibilities for the production and reproduction of present and future citizens are being assumed by a new generation. The reward is the recognition of the individual as a full and proper member of society. There is the underlying notion of a bargain struck, and a new but anticipated and expected contract made between society and a rising generation.

Thus whilst the tension between romantic love and the suitability of a prospective spouse has long been recognized in modern Western societies, recession can raise this problem more acutely. What if a daughter wanted to marry someone without a job, but someone who was not only pleasant and caring but also eager for work? Some parents were quite sure that the situation would not arise for them. They and their daughters were confident that a jobless young man would not become a fiancé. Yet, as some had discovered, unemployment could strike unexpectedly. Some attempted to reconcile the two demands: one mother who said that she would discourage any such attachment reluctantly added that she might accept the situation if she were sure the boy was seriously looking for work. In other words, she sought evidence that the work ethic was still present. But, as Mrs Hewitt observed, when a daughter is over 18:

> You can't say, 'Don't go out with him, and don't go out with him.' You just sort of hope that . . . they meet somebody decent, and when they do settle down it's somebody who has got . . . some qualifications maybe . . . or even a decent job. It doesn't have to be a fabulous job.

Thus economic recession upset the expected progression to this stage of the life course. Unemployment, sudden loss of job, sub-employment and the prevailing uncertainty of job security for those in work influenced thoughts about marriage and family. Parents wondered what would happen to their children. The knowledge that time does not stand still and that 'life has to go on after all' implies not only a sense of the transience of the life stages which could be lost for ever, but also the feeling that perhaps people will continue to marry or cohabit and have children despite adverse circumstances.[5] There is little evidence yet. Wallace (1987) found that by the age of 21, about one-fifth of the young people she studied on Sheppey had married, although the majority had left home. In only four of the thirty-two couples who were married or cohabiting, however, were both partners unemployed; in two others the woman was employed and the man unemployed. One reason given for cohabitation rather than marriage was that parents did not approve of their daughters marrying unemployed men and discouraged them from doing so.

In sum, therefore, the ways people became recognized as citizens, through work and marriage, were interrupted. People felt outside the normal hum and flow of life. Several used the term 'limbo' – the place where forgotten and unwanted things collect. Several referred to being in a backwater, forgotten, thrown away. 'You just don't know when it's going to *end*,' said Mrs Hamilton, 'You just don't see any sort of future' (emphasis in original).

TIME WORLDS

As well as disrupting long-term plans, economic recession pene-trated the minutiae of daily life contributing to the disorientation in personal well-being and family relationships already described. Much has been written of the importance of paid employment in providing a structure to a person's day (Jahoda *et al.* 1972). However, work in the public domain of paid employment also impinges upon the domestic organization of the household, pro-ducing family routines or schedules which not only provide a material order but also sustain and symbolize a moral order, participation in which contributes to social solidarity. Unemployed people could find themselves marginalized from this ordering of time, living in different time worlds and unable to share in collective, time-marked activities.

Time is an ambiguous and elastic entity (Wallman 1984). Amongst the Newcastle families, unemployment could give rise to disorientating contrasts and contradictions which were reflected in lack of personal well-being. Those who had been in work, whose days had been tightly structured, and who had experienced time as a scarce resource insufficient for their personal ends, now had time in abundance. Yet, as Jahoda *et al.* (1972) noted, paradoxically this expanse of time strangely contracts so that the unemployed, with more time, do less even of those activities which their small incomes still allow for. As Mr Hewitt observed of his son:

> He became – depressive, quiet, really quiet. . . .[T]he little things he used to do he stopped doing . . . and he basically just started to lounge around all the time, never take much interest in anything other than his football. He had no other interests. Even stopped listening to his music that much.

There was also the direct contradiction of wasted time with its importance as a strand of the still-pervasive work ethic by which time is seen as a priceless and irreplaceable resource. This contradiction, perhaps, accounts in part for the irritation parents felt when their unemployed children spent the day 'hanging on the walls' or idling their time away watching the television. The remarks made by the father in the above quotation were prefaced by observations which illustrate the tension between the imperative of the work ethic and the erosion of well-being:

> To be quite honest, I think I was a bit of a hard task master. . . .I couldn't understand it. . . .I don't think I was fully aware of what the situation was, how bad it was. My cry used to be, 'If you want work you'll find it. The man that wants to work, he'll find a job'. . . . But this is not my thesis, this is something that was drilled into me as a lad . . . so I used to get onto him a little bit in *that* way, and . . . gradually as time went on . . . as the weeks turned into months, and the months turned to years, and I realized how bad the situation was. And another thing, I think the overall factor was that I watched the change in him. He became morbid, miserable, hard to communicate with, bad-tempered and at the finish, I think it was hurting me more than it was hurting him. That was the situation just before he started working (emphasis in original).

That unease arose from this contradictory expansion and contraction of the day – described by Jahoda *et al.* (1972) as a return to a more primitive and less differentiated experience of time – was evident in the attempts by some young people to impose their own structure upon the hours. Geoffrey Lewis, for example, forced himself to take part in a range of activities for the unemployed. Margaret Hills' older brother began to monitor his time, his perceptions and use of it, by keeping a detailed diary and allocating activities to predetermined time slots.

As Jahoda *et al.* (1972) also noted, the situation produced contrasting time worlds within the family. The disjunctions created were highlighted amongst the Newcastle families by the issue of staying in bed. For some, the generally accepted scheduling of time in broad conformity with others in the pattern of sleeping and waking lost its hold. Time patterns could be almost completely reversed. 'Sleeping all day and awake all night', as Mrs Hamilton put it, 'which causes a lot of friction. I mean, we're going to bed to get up for work next morning. . . .They tend to sort of keep people awake.' For others, a day starting in the late afternoon could lead to jibes and raise a sense of shock with oneself:

It used to be terrible, two o'clock. I used to think to myself,
'Jesus, half the day's passed away.' . . . Before you knew it, it
was bloody tea-time. She [his mother] used to say, 'Oh, here
he comes, the lazy git.'

(Stuart Drake)

'Staying in bed' was, however, charged with deeper complexities
than the upset and anger when others' sleep was disturbed. The
proximity of people who occupied different time worlds raised
contradictions for both. There was the anomaly between the
morality of being up in the morning at a 'decent' time and
having no work to go to, and the inconvenience such moral
conformity might cause for those who had to meet their own
journeys' externally imposed deadlines. The tightly scheduled
business of a family getting itself off to work and school each
morning was vividly revealed in the diaries; one less to account
for in terms of waking, bathroom use, space and energy of other
family members. 'I used to let them lie, one less out of the road,
isn't it?' said Mrs Robson.

This situation, however, created other contradictions. To those
in work, the unemployed could raise the confused emotions of
irritation if they were up, envy if they stayed in bed, and pity over
their lack of employment. Moreover, the practices and moralities of
family life could be upset. Mrs Robson's initial insistence that her
unemployed sons got up at a 'reasonable' hour was undermined for
two reasons: first by the illogicality of forcing her sons out of bed
either for a futile search for work or to face an empty day; second,
because their mere presence disrupted her daily routine which was
organized around domestic chores, caring for her elderly father,
and her part-time job: 'It affects you more if they're in the house
each day because it knocks you out of your routine. You're sort
of hanging back for them.' Thus the moral order of adherence
to a work ethic, symbolized in early rising, interfered with the
material order of the household, posing a dilemma only resolved
when Mrs Robson's husband obtained labouring work for both
boys. In Douglas' (1975) terms, therefore, the unemployed –
whether in bed or out of bed – were, literally, matter out of
place, posing threats to the established and morally defined order
of the household.

As well as producing contrasting time worlds within the same
household, the temporal order in the use of household space was

103

also disturbed. The effect of young people's unemployment upon families with large houses has not been studied. The Newcastle families, however, were severely limited in their resource of space. They lived in small houses or flats – most owned by the local authority, some privately owned. Living rooms were small, and frequently children shared a bedroom. The provision of such mass public and private accommodation has rested upon particular assumptions about the family–household in our society. Housing policy has been informed by an image of the family as one comprising two adults with two young children. Given that children grow, this has been implicitly rationalized through assumptions about family time, the assumption that a similar family life-cycle pattern is followed by all; in this case, that following a relatively brief period when pressure on space is particularly acute, by their late teens to mid-twenties, the young will by and large have left the parental home to establish homes of their own.

A further assumption concerns the daily and weekly temporal rhythms in the use of household space. These are geared to the industrial time of the working day and week. Thus, apart from early child-rearing years, dwellings may be largely empty during the day – family members at school, college or work – with evenings, nights and weekends as the periods of most intensive use. Physical pressure on space as children reach adolescence and young adulthood is tempered for many parents by the expectation that space will be released when children leave the nest.

However unsatisfactory and restricted the accommodation, the hours of paid employment outside the home provided a patterned use of space in the days and weeks of domestic life. Unemployment disrupted this pattern, producing effects which ranged from over-crowding and friction to isolation and estrangement. Sheer pressure on space could cause problems, especially if several members of the family were unemployed. As Mr Clark observed, 'These houses were built as workers' houses, out all day, not for leisure.' Irritation and friction led to Sandra Cross leaving home to live with her married sister. As her sister explained:

It was with them being on top of each other all the time, you see, with her being out of work. They were spending too much company together, all the time being there, in the house and everything. It just came to a big fight and she left.

The recent changes in social policy, described earlier, which lengthen the years of dependency upon parents are likely to intensify such problems.

Some families adopted strategies to ease these physical constraints. For example, Mrs Hills – a mother of three adult children, two of whom had been unemployed together – delayed her return from work in the evenings. 'These houses weren't built for five adults', remarked her husband. He not only wondered when his 26-year-old son would contemplate marriage but whether his younger, unemployed son would even be able to. He had looked forward to the time when his children would leave home, but had found that unemployment and a poor labour market intensified and extended the period of pressure upon family living space. The disruption of the young person's expectations thus rebounds in a very material way upon the normal expectations of middle-aged parents.

In contrast to this kind of pressure, which could be present all day in families where several members were unemployed, the unemployed could find themselves isolated if the rest of the family were all out at work or school. The estrangement produced by both these situations is taken up below.

The unemployed were out of place and out of time in other ways. Temporal symmetry denotes the synchronization of the activities of different individuals and the tendency to do many things in our lives at the same time as others, creating, thereby, a sense of social solidarity (Zerubavel 1981). Exclusion from collective patterns and rhythms can be stigmatizing and painful. In the Benedictine Order a common means of punishing a monk was to separate his activities temporally from those of the rest of the community – for example, eating meals three hours after rather than together with the others. Zerubavel's (1981) example finds echoes in the experience of the unemployed as they lose their place in being part of things.

Being part of things is not confined to the activities and social relationships of work; it includes leisure, appearance and the numerous and apparently trivial activities which constitute the daily round of family life. The unemployed young people in this study had not merely lost the structure imposed by a working day. Not going out to work meant, ironically, that they were not part of the mass deprived of time, who had to squeeze shopping into lunch hours, who were too tired to go out in the evening. They had time in abundance, time which had to be wasted in order to be filled: going for a cup of coffee with an unemployed daughter, lengthening the time taken to reach the job centre by taking a sister-in-law's child in a push-chair. Neither were they part of the collective flow of daily life. They did not, for example, stand at bus queues or get crushed on public transport at peak travel times. They were outcasts from the solidarity arising from collective temporalities.

Temporal symmetry was disturbed in another domain. As noted, unemployed members could not easily participate in those schedules of family life prescribed by industrial time and which produce their own intimacies. Geoffrey Lewis, who listened from his bed to his family's early morning routines, observed: 'Everyone's left for work canny early, 7 o'clock, 8 o'clock, 9 o'clock. I can hear them all talking and that. There's nowt *really* for me to get up for. . . . Like there's nowt [no jobs] gannin' (emphasis in original). Nor could they participate in the family discourse of teasing and chatter. Even in caring families, unemployed members would increasingly retreat physically and psychologically from such family intimacies. 'He just lived in a world of his own. . . . [H]e just wasn't bothered with anything or anybody,' said Mr Bryant; 'I'm afraid she tended to go into her room quite a bit,' observed Mrs McGuinness. Her dilemma regarding her daughter staying in bed late suggests the psychologically outcast state behind such withdrawal. 'Well, I wasn't very happy about it . . . and then I just thought, "How would I have felt at her age?" And I thought, "God, I would do the same myself. I would crawl up in a blanket and hide myself."' Her daughter's lowered resistance to horseplay and teasing had led Mrs McGuinness to 'speak to' her married older sons, and when her daughter eventually obtained work she observed, 'She's one of the crowd now . . . and when her brothers heard she'd started work, they were picking her up [in the air], you know. . . .'

The unemployed had lost access to other time-structured resources which foster belonging. For example, living in different time worlds limited their contribution to family conversation. This was especially marked at those points in the family day, tea-time for example, when members returning from the outside world of work pooled their separate, individual experiences, 'moaned about work'; but the undifferentiated and uneventful time of those who stayed at home was already public knowledge. Geoffrey Lewis contrasted the period on a YOP scheme with his present situation:

106

It was like, just like being part of the, . . . like closer to the family . . . like talking about things that happened and things like that. When they come in now they know, like, all I've been doing is sitting about. . . . There's not much to talk about when I've been sitting about. I could bring up conversation when I come in from work easier, much easier.

Finally, the inability to share in temporal patterns was an aspect of the uncertainties surrounding expectations of the future. As noted, an individual's life course comprises strands of several careers, sometimes coinciding, sometimes conflicting (Brannen 1987), but the sense of there being a 'proper' time for each stage of the family or domestic career, particularly marriage, is underpinned by an expectation of its coincidence with an appropriate stage in the employment career. Unemployment throws these career timetables (Zerubavel 1981) out of phase. In addition, however, unemployment may deny people the option of 'settling down' and thus potentially marginalizes individuals from the progression of their generation through historical time.

THE LANGUAGE OF DISORDER

In this chapter on the disorder which job insecurities and unemployment set in train, account must be taken of the language and idiom through which people described their situations.

The general malaise which unemployment could produce was noted earlier. However, whilst people did not consider themselves to be ill, the recurrence of the word 'sick' was striking. Young people were 'sick of being on the dole', 'sick of seeing the same four walls' (Annette Maynard after four years' unemployment), 'sick of enquiring [about] jobs and getting nowhere in a hurry' (Kevin Ryan), 'pig-sick of being unemployed' (Neil Peters). They noted how a boyfriend might be 'a bit sick if he didn't have a job' and how a girlfriend was 'getting sick of us going on about it' (Neil Peters). Mr Phillips recounted his reaction to his son's redundancy letter: 'He said, "I've got a letter," and he showed it. You know, you feel *sick*' (emphasis in original).

Closely allied with expressions of sickness were those of boredom and of being fed up. 'I'm sick, mam, I'm fed up, I couldn't stand it,' said one of Mrs McGuire's older daughters at the thought of remaining unemployed. The unemployed could be 'bored out of me mind' or be 'not really depressed, just bored, you know, sick', a remark from Geoffrey Lewis, attempting to structure his day and who felt that during unemployment his increased involvement in fitness training had improved his physical health.

Lakoff and Johnson (1981) argue that the metaphors through which we interpret and shape our lives are grounded in our experiences. Metaphors of sickness, boredom and being fed up have related meanings of surfeit, oppression and disgust with over-abundance, of being thoroughly tired and weary of a thing; of being deeply affected by some strong feeling, producing effects similar to those of physical ailment; of sickness or disorder by overfeeding. These definitions are founded in the disorder and abuse of one of the body's systems, in this case the digestive tract.

Surfeit, oppression, disorder and abuse in the lives of those living through recession were intimately related to their experience of time and place. The unemployed young people in the study suffered from several surfeits: of a sense of rejection, of low income but also of time. Not only had they too much, but time itself was disordered, affecting them and intruding upon others. They were not in the right place at the right time. They were out of phase with those rhythms and flows of life which, in our society, are considered to be normal. They felt abused, unfairly treated by the wider society.

The endemic issue of staying in bed can be viewed from this perspective. The tensions and paradoxes created have been noted; the range of rationales included laziness, being in the way, no point in getting up, and so forth. Yet, to stay in bed is a legitimate part of the sick role. Sick people stay in bed.[6] Here, however, it produced a mixture of censure, sympathy and an awareness that it could actually be bad for you, 'lead to bad habits' for life and to a continued disjunction with the rest of the world. It could be, however, that retreat to bed was not mere over-indulgence but a sign of the underlying disorder into which the unemployed were thrust, leading eventually, perhaps, to a more recognizable breakdown in health. The mother's empathy with her daughter, noted earlier, alluded to this; wounded animals would crawl away and hide either to aid their recovery or to die.

The metaphor of sickness also emerged in other instances which suggested the incipient adoption of a sick role and with it a latent hierarchy which colours the relationships between employed and unemployed. Visits to the unemployed were described in the idiom of sick-visiting: 'There was two girls who work where I'm working now, and they really, they were really good. They kept coming and seeing us and all that' (Margaret Hills). Fagin and Little (1984) argue that, because unstigmatized, a sick role is easier to bear than that of unemployment. The sick role, however, has other important dimensions. It was not that the girl was ill but rather that the adoption of the passivity, gratefulness and subordination contained in the comment, and which characterize the good patient, possibly helped her relationship with employed friends.

Metaphors which structure our thought and action form coherent systems across physical, cultural and intellectual domains of concepts (Lakoff and Johnson 1981). The discrete metaphors of sickness were embedded in a text replete with words and phrases depicting the subordination of the individual, both of the inner self and in relationships with others. Several appear in the quotations cited; a few examples of such phrases will suffice here: 'down in the dumps', 'gets you down', 'pulls you down', 'gets you down inside', 'pulls your confidence down', 'feeling bad', 'sets me back', '[employed friends] feel above you, they suddenly change', 'degrading at this age the feeling that nobody wants you', 'stripped of their dignity', 'it's sad', 'just idling away', 'stuck on the dole', 'on the scrapheap', 'broke her heart'.

Many of these reflect the elements of Lakoff and Johnson's (1981) system of UP-DOWN spatialization metaphors. As they note, general well-being – happiness, health, life, control and status – has the general orientation of being up. 'Health and life are up; sickness and death are down. . . . Serious illness forces us physically to lie down. When you are ill you are physically down' (Lakoff and Johnson 1981: 297).

In using these phrases, people were expressing the meaning unemployment held for them. They were intimating the effect upon their inner selves and on their relationships with others and with society in general.

CONCLUSION

At all times people seek to impose some sense of order upon the daily pattern of their lives and on the shape of their future. Although surrounded by change, both in their personal histories and in the world about them, they manage to achieve a sense of stability. Pertinently for the age group at the centre of this study, normal adult life is perceived as a period of settling down and it is to this that the life events of the teenage years and early adulthood are seen as a prelude. This chapter showed the depth to which a poor local labour market could undermine this sense of order and progression. Again it should be said that the belief – whether true or false – that regions of endemic unemployment, such as the North-East, are able to carry the costs more easily than places where unemployment is a relatively new phenomenon, does not detract from the disorientation and disturbance experienced by the Newcastle families.

Order in people's lives was not merely a matter of superior personal organization on the part of some, but was constructed out of resources people had. In addition to economic, social, cultural and emotional capital, time and space were particularly important. It was the lack of paid employment, however, which dominated and upset the fragile order which had been constructed. The loss of well-being and family harmony were underpinned by disjunctions in time and space as schedules were disrupted and the unemployed were excluded from collective time. The different time worlds of the employed and unemployed meant that the unemployed were both out of time and out of place. The language of sickness which people used in describing their lives suggests the depth at which such disjunction is felt and the changed status in relation to others. At a subconscious level, the language hints at the underlying changes in social structure, factors which can eventually lead to physical disorder in health.

The economic disorder of the wider society created such social disorder; a disordered public domain impinged upon the private, socially and psychologically marginalizing individuals and penetrating psychological and physical well-being. However, the character of a society is not solely the product of external forces and systems acting upon the individual, for how the individual or group responds reverberates back upon that society. The earlier chapters described how family members drew upon their material and other resources to meet the challenge. The next chapter looks more closely at extension of disorder into norms and values, and how the responses here contribute in turn to the societal ambience.

5

THE MORAL COMMUNITY

INTRODUCTION

Values and social norms, beliefs about how life should be conducted, underpinned the daily lives of the Newcastle families, the long-term expectations and hopes of the young people and their parents' hopes for them. This thread, of course, has run through all the chapters. The description of the labour market in Chapter Two, for example, drew upon the implicit assumptions about familial obligation and labour market norms. Chapter Three showed how beliefs about work could inform the practices of parenting; and the implicit and explicit recognition of the norm of independence was the motif of the chapter. Similarly, in Chapter Four, the notion of order which people held implies the presence of social norms governing ideas about time and place, where people should be and when they should be there, whether this referred to the physical space of the home or the particular staging posts of life's journey.

This next chapter focuses on values. It looks at the mediating processes within the family by which values are transmitted, sustained, prioritized and undermined in times of economic change; in other words, it attempts to identify some of the effects of a poor labour market on the moral community. Not all can be included here, but the values which have been selected for examination – fairness and familism – seemed particularly salient. Around these are issues of equity and equality, reciprocity and trust, the work ethic, gender, and power.

THE CHALLENGE TO VALUES

Kornhauser (1960) has noted that in periods of social change, people are jolted out of their social niches, and here the uncertainties of the restructuring labour market produced social and cultural discontinuities. Fluctuating employment statuses, anxiety about the security of jobs held and, in some cases, lengthy spells of unemployment upset both daily schedules and all those life career strands which constitute the life course. Not only, however, were the expected patterns of people's lives disturbed, but also disturbed were the values and social norms which coloured people's attempts to shape their lives. The changes in the labour market both exposed latent values and challenged them. First, it seemed that some deeply held values were being eroded; second, contradictions between highly regarded values in the culture became more explicit. People had, somehow, to mediate and cope with this in their family relationships.

The many shared values present in a society do not form a coherent system,[1] although a work ethic and a norm of independence may, in fact, be complementary. If the attributes associated with the work ethic – reliability, good timekeeping and so forth – lead to paid employment, the ensuing economic rewards open up the possibilities of independence in the private sphere of leisure, consumption and domestic life; although there are complexities here since, for most people, paid employment means the loss of independence and control over time and activity in the public domain of the workplace. Gender, of course, introduces further complexities.

As well as such balances of gains and losses, however, social change exposes more direct contradictions. While in some circumstances the oppositions may be cloaked, in others they are not only brought to the forefront of attention, but uncomfortable choices have to be made. In an economy where jobs are plentiful, familism and equity, for example – two major values in our culture – can be accommodated; when jobs are scarce the competing claims of these values become apparent. In such circumstances the priority society accords to familism is revealed even more clearly than before in such established practices as 'speaking for' a son or daughter and in such comments as 'you've got to look after your own'.

Similarly, in an economy with a high demand for labour, the waters may close over gender categories and social status distinctions amongs men. In contrast, when jobs are scarce, the latent categories through which people organize their interpretation of the world may rise to the surface and influence judgements and decisions which intimately affect people's lives.

THE FAMILY AS MEDIATOR

The response families make when values and social norms are challenged raises the issue of the family's role in social change. Whilst many studies chart the effect of social change upon families, it is also claimed that the family is not exclusively a dependent variable merely responding to changes in its environment. For example, the family – or more specifically here the social norms and practices of family life – can directly influence the composition of the labour force and employers' scheduling of work time, noted in the previous chapter. The 'nursery' or 'tea-time' shift, most productively drawn upon by some employers, is a direct response to familistic norms which say that the care of young children takes priority over paid employment in a mother's life. In another case, McLoughlin's (1973) study of Italians in Buffalo showed how immigrant families selectively entered those sectors of the labour market which sustained their traditional values and norms.[2]

The earlier chapters showed how the changes in the labour market, particularly the local labour market, had extensive repercussions upon family relationships and organization, producing uncertainty and disorientations. Response to the changing environment, however, was not passive. Families mobilized their collective and individual resources to sustain threatened values. Furthermore, in the interests of their own survival, they made selective decisions about which values to sustain and in what context. Priorities were made in view of their loyalties and obligations – obligations, it should be said, that society vests in the family – to care for its members, particularly the young. The outcome of such decisions, it can be argued, does not remain within the confines of family life; changes in emphasis amongst a culture's values which are made by families become, in turn, part of the embracing culture.

It is through such familial processes that social change is mediated. Land (1979) has noted how, paradoxically, the family both inhibits and facilitates social change because of its key position as the institution for creating and structuring continuities from one generation to the next. This tension between the past and future was revealed in the way values were articulated within families. The desire to retain the established and expected patterns of family relationships and routines of daily life competed with the necessity to prepare children to cope in a changing world.

THE NOTION OF FAIRNESS

Much of the sense of dislocation and change cohered around the notion of fairness. Like all values and social norms, fairness is an ideal. Nonetheless, it was invoked in descriptions and anecdotes in response to questions about jobs, labour market histories and family life. Fairness was a yardstick against which parents and young people measured what was happening around them. They were not, of course, unique in calling upon this concept, since a concept of fairness is dominant in our culture. 'A fair day's work for a fair day's pay' is a cry of both employer and employee; we refer to 'fair play'; and references to fairness, unfairness and moral outrage abound in the daily press. Just as Gouldner (1960) has postulated a universal norm of reciprocity, Moore (1978), in his analysis of injustice, suggests a related social norm of fairness, arguing that moral outrage is a universal response to injustice; individuals know when they have had a 'raw deal'. He argues that 'the fundamental idea behind popular conceptions of justice and injustice, fairness and unfairness is the conception of "reciprocity" or "mutual obligation"' (Moore 1978: 508–9), the essential component of which is not based upon force, fear or fraud. The notion of reciprocity is one 'where services and favours, trust and affection, in the course of mutual exchanges are ideally expected to find some rough balancing out' (Moore 1978: 509). Such reciprocity does not mean that a return for any service or gift has to be immediate or identical. Furthermore, what is reciprocated is decided by the reciprocator (Blau 1964). However, whilst Gouldner postulates that a universal norm of reciprocity leads people to behave in certain ways, Moore is suggesting that a norm of fairness enables us to recognize when that 'rough balancing out' has been achieved.

When obligations are not reciprocated, this breaking of social rules produces a sense of unfairness and consequently anger and moral outrage in the injured party. It can occur both in situations of equality and of hierarchy. In the first type, individuals or groups, perceiving each other as equals, will experience a sense of unfairness if advantage accrues to one and not to all – for example, members of the same economic groups, work grades or siblings (although there are also circumstances, such as that referred to in Chapter Four, when sibling hierarchies come into play). In the second, hierarchical type, subordinate groups perceive unfairness in their treatment by their superiors. For example, citizens may perceive the actions of the government to be unfair, employees the actions of their employers, and children the actions of their parents. In such unequal relationships the authority of dominant groups is felt to be legitimate when the obligations are fulfilled. Thus, Moore (1978) argues, in return for compliance (although not necessarily acceptance), dominant groups are obliged to supply commodities and services such as protection, security and not an equal but a tolerable distribution of resources. Amongst the Newcastle families, for example, there was a feeling that the government or 'society' had opted out of its responsibilities towards the young.

Two further characteristics of reciprocity – its latent and its dynamic qualities – were important in understanding the interaction between labour market experience and cultural values as they were expressed amongst these families. Reciprocity rests upon the implicit social contract of unwritten, unspoken and unspecified mutual obligations and understandings (Durkheim 1957). In this, precedent and tradition play a part, and in a stratified society there are limits to what either subordinate or dominant groups can legitimately do. However, while all parties recognize the existence of such limits, their precise location is unknown. Individuals and groups, in seeking to further their interests, test and discover where these boundaries lie. As Marie Davis said of her employer's demand for unpaid overtime: 'He really went too far.' The terms of this implicit contract are thus constantly under renegotiation. In periods of social change, with the ensuant redistribution of power, this process of renegotiation becomes more visible as former boundaries, denoted by custom and practice, are breached. Severe problems of unemployment for young people and the social and cultural dislocation they experience reveal the limits which some groups will accept; simultaneously, they show the advantages in the bargaining process which accrue to those in control, whether employers or parents.

Finally, embedded in the notion of reciprocity are those of trust and risk. Reciprocities cannot develop if people do not trust each other. Blau describes how trust develops:

> Typically . . . exchange relations evolve in a slow process, starting with minor transactions in which little trust is required because little risk is involved. . . .By discharging their obligations for services rendered, if only to produce inducements for the supply of more assistance, individuals demonstrate their trustworthiness, and the gradual expansion of mutual services is accompanied by a parallel growth in mutual trust.
>
> (Blau 1964: 94)

Trust is important to the functioning of a society. It is also central to parenting. Baier (1985:61) has drawn attention to 'the complex network of a great variety of trust which structures our moral relationship with our fellows', pointing out how this ranges from those entrusted with great powers of coercion and decision making to the trust placed in those who care for dependants. She argues that people have to learn about what she calls 'appropriate trust'; it is possible to be too trusting as well as untrustworthy. She suggests that, 'if there is a *main* support to this network it is the trust we place in those who respond to the trust of new members of the moral community, namely to children, and prepare them for new forms of trust' (emphasis in original) (Baier 1985: 61).

The idea of trust was a recurrent theme in the interviews. The young people were in that interstitial stage between parental control and self-control; the locus of this control is apparent when we make the distinction between uncontrolled children and irresponsible adults. Parents frequently said how they now had to trust their children: they were beginning to relinquish the reins even if they were uncertain about the outcome and they only hoped that the way they had brought up their children had taken root. This was apparent in the concern about a sense of responsibility and the reliability they hoped to see in their children, noted in Chapter Three. This notion of trust was important, for in the changing labour market the complex of trust itself was changing. Society entrusts parents with the job of rearing and training persons so that they can be trusted in various ways. However, there were changes taking place which undermined the assumptions which had underpinned this teaching.

116

Fairness and the labour market

The notions of reciprocity and of an implicit social contract were prominent in people's descriptions and interpretations of their changing social world. A view of a fair contract with an employer and the reciprocities of mutual exchange in social life in general were illuminated by Mr Hughes' views, spelled out in a whole range of relationships with regard to employment. He believed in 'a fair day's work for a fair day's pay'. He saw himself as a good worker, aware of his value to an employer, and was prepared to work hard for a proper reward. 'They need me as much as I need them. . . . They want their pound of flesh but they pay you a decent wage.' The element of trust implicit in reciprocity, particularly in view of its place in parenting, was exemplified in his practice of allowing his children access to his wallet; in return they would leave IOUs which, he said, were always honoured.

In his discussion of work, Mr Hughes made frequent reference to 'the carrot' as the reward for effort or for going beyond the bounds of duty in what was his view of the normal social contract. For others, however, such carrots were gradually becoming mean-ingless, mere symbols of promises unfulfilled or, in harsher instances, being replaced by the stick. It suggested that former implicit understandings were being renegotiated. For example, one young woman, an office junior, had been encouraged by her employer by the promise of promotion to qualify as a typist. When she qualified, however, promotion was only given when she asked for a reference for another job. Not all, however, have another job to go to when promises and obligations are not fulfilled. This is not to say that poor work relationships do not exist when jobs are easily available. In such circumstances, however, employees are more able to leave and find more conducive employment, and a limited pool of available labour is more likely to temper employers' behaviour.

While Mr Hughes' view of the mutuality of reciprocity in social and economic life was particularly lucid and systematic, others indicated a general awareness of social norms being eroded or ignored. A sense of injustice was conveyed in discussions of young people's relationships with employers and prospective employers, their experience of government schemes and their exposure to unemployment. As well as obligations not fulfilled, people drew attention to what they saw as major abuses and exploitation.

The complaints and stories, referred to earlier in Chapter Two, revealed the levels at which people sensed that an erosion of labour market norms was taking place. They ranged from the disregard of the common courtesy of responding to letters of application and broken promises to deception about job tenure, illegal practices and the loss of legal rights following changes in the structure of the labour market. The following examples illustrate this range.

Apparently trivial points stuck in people's minds. Mrs McGuinness recalled her daughter's reaction when promises were not kept; such seemingly mundane neglect of the conventional civilities could be potent reminders of powerlessness and rejection:

> She wrote away after a lot of jobs and I think that wasn't much help to her, and they said they would let her know and they never did. I said to her dad, 'It's very degrading at that age to think that nobody wants you.' She even put stamped addressed envelopes in and I thought, 'Well, they could have decency, wrote "no" on the paper and re-posted it or picked the phone up and said, "She's not wanted," or "She's not good enough," even.' I think it's terrible for them. I thank God I'm not a kid just starting, anyway.

Mr Mitchell described his frustrated anger at broken promises. On leaving school his son had obtained work at a printers but was laid off along with twenty others after an urgent order for the Royal Wedding had been rushed through:

> I went and had a word with the manager. He just made excuses, you know. But there was nothing I could do about it. I was mad at the time because he had promised him a full-time job and nothing came of it.

Peter Hamilton recalled how he felt he had been deceived by a past employer, and how a commitment to work went unrewarded:

> It was supposed to be a proper job, a month's trial I was on. They took three of wer on and after the month they got rid of two of wer and kept one on. I think they took three on with the intention that they weren't gonna keep three on, just one. Two of wer went and we hadn't done nowt wrong, yer know, we worked.

Michael Howard had worked in a small garage business which had closed down. Mrs Howard described the illegality and unfairness in her son's experience:

The fella he was working for neither paid his tax nor his insurance even though it was stopped out of his pay. And now he's got to pay £75 back so he can get his old age pension when he's an old man for what somebody else has done. That man was earning a decent wage and then to do something like that to the two fellas who was keeping his business going.

The anger in her voice as she described this breach of trust conveyed how deeply such injustice was felt. Furthermore, many parents could still recall the casual employment which characterized the shipbuilding industry in the past and recognized the loss of legal rights which could accompany the present deteriorating employment conditions (Spence 1985). As Mr Hamilton observed, 'If a man is employed on a temporary basis he won't have to be paid redundancy money. He's on a lower wage for a start which is another way the firms cash in.'

Whether or not harsher patterns than in the recent past were, in fact, colouring these relationships between dominant and subordinate groups in the labour market, many people certainly felt that they were. Moreover, whilst there were criticisms of the relationship between traditionally competing interest groups of employer and employee, there were other fierce criticisms of the treatment young people were subject to on government schemes. This and the attitude of the State in general towards young people evoked a moral condemnation of both State and government.

Complaints were made about conditions of employment. Mrs Harris said she would refuse to permit her child to take a place on a government training scheme which, she had heard, involved shift work, for £25 a week when fares cost £3 a day: 'and doing *shift* work. I thought it was diabolical. I wouldn't have let mine *go*. I would have told them straight, "No".' In some cases young people, Bryan Jones for example, had been offered training opportunities which did not materialize, while others felt they had been misled about the chance of permanent work when the scheme came to an end. Several parents felt the whole rationale of the government special measures was a deception on young people. Mr Clark, whose son was still out of work despite completing a computer course at an ITEC (Information Technology Centre), remembered the Prime Minister's words as she officially opened the centre:

This was her when she opened it, 'After twelve months' training here these young people will go straight on to get a job.' It's just all a load of rubbish. It's just one big kid from start to finish. After two months he had learned what they were gonna learn him down there and the rest of the time he was just hanging around. They even had him painting and things like that, and then they wanted him to gan rock-climbing and stupid things like that. What he wanted was a job and that was one thing what they never come up with.

The implicit contract between a government and people and the sense of obligation and duty abandoned was voiced by Mr Hamilton. He was very angry about youth unemployment. Both his sons had had difficulty in finding work and the younger one was still unemployed. In his view, 'What the government's doing to the youth of this country is absolutely criminal. It's no good saying that they can't find these lads work, work can be created.'

The work ethic

By definition the family mediates changes in its environment. But the way people dealt with unemployment and the apparent erosion of social norms which governed labour market behaviour had repercussions for other values.

Efforts were made to sustain the status quo. Parental interventions with employers, for example, were attempts to stem the encroachment upon what were seen as rights. Thus, like Mr Mitchell, some parents intervened to ensure adherence to the implicit contract between employer and their offspring. As noted earlier, Marie Davis' father complained when her employer regularly kept her working until 10 o'clock at night and did not pay overtime rates. As she described it:

> From 8 in the morning you had no choice, he just expected me to stay. Oh my parents were mad, they were livid. Sometimes they used to phone up and tell him what they thought of him 'cos he went a bit beyond a joke.

In another case a father refused to leave the employer's office until the reference to which his son was entitled was written.

Similarly, generous parental subsidies to young people and payment for major household maintenance tasks were material and symbolic assertions that it was 'proper' for young people 'to have money in their pockets and to be out enjoying themselves at their age'; it also implied a dereliction of duty and unfulfilled obligation to young people on the part of society and the State. As Mrs Robson observed, 'You've got to compensate in something.'

There were, however, dilemmas. Parents were frequently aware of their powerlessness. Thus in the case referred to above, although Mr Mitchell received the reference he demanded for his son, his son had already left the firm. In other cases, there was the problem that a query about work conditions or about an employer's intention to honour a generally acknowledged right to an age-related pay rise might precipitate dismissal.

Unemployment also posed what Douglas (1966) has described as threats to the structure of beliefs and moralities. The threats here were to those beliefs and moralities associated with the idea of work, described in detail in Chapter Three, and to the place of work in people's lives. In circumstances where most young people are unable to enter the labour force without experiencing either some unemployment or difficulties in obtaining work, the work ethic – an important value which, as Chapter Three showed, underpinned many aspects of parenting – may take on a new and more conspicuous significance. The term work ethic is used here to indicate a moral belief that work, especially of the kind performed in return for wages, has intrinsic merit over other forms of activity and (except where other imperatives intervene, such as those relating to age, gender or the social status which wealth confers) should be undertaken by all those capable of it. The paradox that such a belief can achieve a renewed ascendancy in the period of high unemployment is easily unravelled, for its relative scarcity alone gives employment an increased value in the eyes of those who perform it as well as those who seek it.

The idea that to have a job made you one of the elite was noted earlier. Here, Mrs Knight sets the experience in the context of changing times and attitudes. Her daughter had been unemployed for a year, but her son who had just left school at 16 had obtained temporary work as a van lad. She explained how she felt when his search for work paid off so quickly:

I think attitudes are changing and people don't expect – I mean I wasn't expecting Colin to end with a job. To get a job, it must be the greatest morale booster. I don't think people appreciated it a few years back when jobs were plenty, but I think now it's got to make you feel quite special. I mean I feel, 'Ooh, I've got to go out to work, I've got to get out of bed this morning. At least if I wasn't working I'd be able to lie in bed for half an hour.' But then you think, 'Gosh! I'm jolly lucky to have a job and to be able to pick up a wage packet at the end of it.'

However, despite the emphasis many parents had placed upon work in the upbringing of their children, unemployment raised anxieties about the fragility of young people's commitment to the idea of work. In other words, there was a fear that 'the bonds', of which Goffman (1968:159) wrote, 'which tie individuals to social entities' – in this case the social entities of work and the work ethic, which had been built into parenting and the routines of family life described in Chapter Three – would wither in a poor and exploitative labour market.

> Involvement in social entities involves commitment and attachment, that is obligations through work, service and sacrifice, along with emotional attachment, feelings of be-longing and identification but there are unwritten under-standings about the limits of commitment and attachment a social entity can claim.
>
> (Goffman 1968: 159)

Parents obviously felt that it was only engagement in paid work which sustained these ties. As noted earlier, Mrs Drake said her son had lost the incentive to work following long years of unemployment. Thus there was the lurking fear that money easy to come by might undermine any will to work that had been instilled. This did not so much apply to the financial and material support which parents gave to their children (although one parent felt he should not still have to subsidize his employed 21-year-old), since some such support is generally expected at this stage. The fear was about the kind of attitude the receipt of state benefit might encourage and the desultory way in which time might be spent.

Mrs Robson's fear about the ease with which young people could fall into a dependent way of life, especially 'if you start off your life not working', was noted in an earlier chapter. Although her self-imposed standards could slip through the sheer physical inconvenience of having her boys around the house all the time, her husband made clear his expectations about how his unemployed sons should spend their day. He wanted them 'out and looking', whether there was work or not.

Thus the encouragement parents gave their children, the nagging, the threats, the irritability when offspring seemed to be constantly watching television or spending long hours in bed, the joking about 'dole wallahs', were not only means of keeping the work ethic buoyant but, from the parents' point of view, attempts to keep at bay the danger which threatened the principles by which they claimed to have ordered their lives and brought up their children. 'Martin'll work because . . . that's just – he's been brought up in a house where you have to work', said Mrs Pearce; and Mrs Matthews' comments on the unemployed were not, perhaps, of generational differences in values (which may indeed exist) but rather evidence of a feeling that widespread youth unemployment may erode existing values and provide the pre-conditions for unwelcome cultural shifts. For in this view the threat posed by unemployment is not so much that the unemployed can survive without working, but that they may be content to do so; that some of them 'are quite happy to get on with it', 'quite content', is more an accusation than an expression of relief that one's conscience need not be disturbed.

The situation thus brings to the fore the tensions inherent in what is perceived to be good parenting. Parents tread a tightrope between compulsion and protectiveness, conflicts between a harshness stemming from concern for the child's own good, a sense that young people should in any case be earning and contributing, and that of love and affection which seeks to ease a child's life. In some cases, these uneasy tensions of parenting were brought into sharp focus. When Phil Matthews left school abruptly at 17, 'naturally we were disappointed, and Dad said, "Right, no work, no home, *out*"' (Mrs Matthews). 'He got his marching orders' (Mr Matthews). Here Mr Matthews' paternal authority was used to effect – Phil obtained unskilled work the next day – but Mrs Matthews' role in averting further conflict over the issue was also evident. She felt 'very sympathetic' towards her son, and, as noted earlier, she stressed that she 'didn't want him and his dad to break over it'.

The pressures applied by parents may not be as strong as the 'rules of avoidance' which, Douglas (1975: 53) argues, make visible the publicly recognized structure of ideas. However,

Mrs Pearce's comments about the shame she would have felt had her son been unemployed, and her embarrassment and confusion (revealed in both what she said and her mode of expression) when, literally, brought face-to-face with the unemployed, are examples of the unease and discomfiture produced when a dominant value is challenged:

> I didn't tell *anyone* that Martin had been given the, er, you know [four months' notice]. Now at one time it wouldn't have bothered me, but nowadays with jobs being difficult, I think it *is*, you do feel a little bit – ooh there's something *wrong*, if you can't *work*, sort of thing, or they can't *get* a job. . . .I thought 'Ooh, Mark [neighbour's son] mustn't be working.' . . . He's a mechanic and I know he's a good mechanic, and I j[ust] don't know, I just find it very embarrassing, the whole, you know, I just never mention . . . when Martin's friends come in the house, I never say, 'Have you got a – any work now?' I just, you know, skim over the subject, don't mention it at all (emphasis in original).

Thus despite the awareness of job scarcity, her thinking about her own child is structured by the displacement effect which characterizes powerful ideologies. Mrs Pearce is tacitly suggesting that she would hold her own son, if unemployed, in some way responsible for his predicament; structural problems and contradictions inherent in the society or system become defined as the personal failings of the victim (Allatt 1981a; Douglas 1975; Mills 1959).

The example also illustrates how the categories through which experience is structured and ordered may confront each other. As well as threatening personal principles, widespread unemployment can bring into the same arena – the home, where warmth and welcome are ideally supposed to await a guest – the category of friendship (people like us) and the category of unemployment (the shameful state with which we do not wish to be contaminated). Mrs Pearce overcame this uncomfortable and distressing ambiguity by ignoring it. Her comments, however – as well as those of parents who kept an anxious eye on their children's friendships, noted in Chapter Three – suggest that unemployment is dangerous pollution in a society where the work ethic is an important value. Consequently, a range of strategies is used to keep it at bay (Douglas 1975).[3]

Cultural ambiguities: equity, equality and gender

The cultural dislocation of economic recession not only makes visible deeply held values, but may also undermine former challenges to the existing social order which have been sustained by other elements in the culture. The social category of gender, and its relationship to equality and equity or fairness, is one such case. Thus the pressure for equal opportunities for women in the late 1960s and 1970s, irrespective of their actual implementation, appeared to be in danger of being overridden by the re-emergence of dormant traditional views of male and female roles, although it should be said that in the North-East traditional beliefs about the respective roles of men and women have always been marked.

According to Douglas, societies can tolerate cultural ambiguity to varying degrees (Douglas 1975). Within a society, however, such toleration may vary over time; in economic recession, as some power bases are eroded and others strengthened, less tolerance may be shown to ambiguities which disturb deeply held classifications. For example, the economic and domestic categories of gender, deeply held although not necessarily immutable or undisputed, are contaminated and threatened by the visible presence of married women in paid work or by men carrying out certain domestic tasks. Cultural intolerance of ambiguity, Douglas argues, finds expression in avoidance, discrimination and pressure to conform. Although now, in the 1990s, demographic changes may mean that women are once again welcomed into the labour market, the manner in which political voice has been given since the early 1980s to the proposition that women return to the home and the discrimination against girls in many government training schemes for young people, both in the ghettoization in terms of work content and, until recently, the few opportunities offered, would seem to uphold this view (Brelsford *et al.* 1982; Cockburn 1987; Rees 1983).

The issue, however, is not simple. In the Newcastle families the idea of fairness emerged as one of the major underlying assumptions of family life, as Backett found in her study of early parenthood (Backett 1982). Fairness, however, does not necessarily imply equality. Indeed, the idea of fairness was both vague and flexible in a way that is characteristic of such generalized values (Backett 1982; Parsons and Bales 1956). Such diffuseness allows the notion of fairness to embrace a wide range of interpretations and behaviours. Thus, in the Newcastle study, whilst some saw fairness as being identical with equality, in other cases fairness was associated with equity. This equity was mediated by a traditional view of gender roles in marriage, by the types of jobs that were available, and by personal circumstances.

Thus, for example, some young women felt it unfair that girls did not have the same opportunities as boys. Margaret Davies commented:

> I think there's more things for *lads* than what there is for lasses. I think they could give a girl a chance as well. And when lads get the opportunity of getting a job first . . . I think that's *wrong*, they should treat war the same (emphasis in original).

Similarly, some parents felt that employment was as important to a girl as to a boy.

For others, however, the issue was more complicated. Mrs Hughes had compassion for all the young unemployed, and her especial concern for boys was noted in chapter four. She saw work and the support of the family as the role of boys and men, 'their whole purpose in life, what they function for'. Others also made a distinction between the significance of unemployment for young men and young women by looking ahead to what unemployment would mean within a marriage. Mr Hewitt, for example, felt unemployment was worse for a lad because, he said, 'if he's unemployed and he gets married how's he gonna manage and all that sort of thing?'

It was, furthermore, a view and a concern which sometimes rebounded upon the control parents exercised over girls. Deem, for example, refers to the constraints fathers impose upon girls' leisure (Deem 1987).[4] In the anxious times of high unemployment this control may intensify. Mrs Davis explained that her husband was stricter with their daughters than their son because, she explained:

> He always says that he worries they're gonna come in and say they're pregnant. I just hope it never happens. I drummed it into them, I've said, 'Think. Think hard, 'cos once you gan that way, supposing the lad's got no job, then what start have you got in life?'

Again the situation abounded with ambiguities. A traditional sense of what was proper could conflict with the limitations within which people's lives were set. Easier access to and more opportunities in women's unskilled work could markedly influence attitudes. The

19-year-old girlfriend of Stephen Woods, unemployed and the mother of his child, was anxious for them to 'get a home together'. She had given up her job on the birth of the baby and at the time of interview each was living in their parents' homes. Stephen said he could look after the child but she did not favour this plan despite their special circumstances:

> I says to him, 'Why should I work?' when he should work. He should support wer, not me support him and the bairn, then meself. Like if he got a job, I would like get a part-time job when she's one or two.
>
> *Stephen*: But you've got a better chance of getting a proper job 'cos you're the lass. Lasses can be on supermarket tills and what have you. You could get a start tomorrow, but they wouldn't start me there with us having a criminal record and that.
>
> *Girlfriend*: I think that's what knocks your jobs back, 'cos you've been in trouble with the police and it's not fair. They've got to give him a chance. He's never been in trouble for years and years.

Whilst this altercation might have reflected her doubts about his capacity to care for the child, and the traditional views expressed used as a defence, the study did include a (childless) couple, the Wests, of which the unemployed husband looked after the house whilst his wife worked. 'Anybody can look after a house,' he said in response to the interviewer's question about what he thought about undertaking domestic tasks. (Details were not taken of how much housework was done, nor the quality of the performance.) Fairness in the division of labour between the sexes is, however, a complex issue. The comments of Caroline Price, a clerical worker, revealed how the ambiguities of equality and gender roles could be shaped by personal experience and family circumstances. Following a statement that she would not want to marry anyone who was unemployed, she described the tortuous strands in her thinking:

> Me brother did that before. They're separated now but she worked all the time and he stayed in the house and did all the cooking and clearing up. I think it's one of the reasons why they separated because I think she started to resent him because he wasn't working. 'You should be the one that's working', type of thing. 'I should be able to maybe stay

off work and do the housework and have a baby.' She
did actually start saying to him, 'I'm not giving you no
money, you're not going out tonight.' And she was the
only place where he could get money from. You know, if
your husband says to you, 'Please give me a fiver so I can
go out', it's not very nice. I think if I did eventually get
married and that, I wouldn't want to work. I think that's
another reason why there's not so many jobs as well, it's
because women do men's jobs these days and I don't think
that's such a good thing after all. Even they are driving the
buses now, women. You don't see many of them mind. I
think I have always seen me mam go out to work and she
has always worked, and then she will come dashing in and
get the tea ready. And me dad, although he does a lot of
things around the house, he always seems to still get that
bit waited on, and I think when me mam's working that's
not right. But if she wasn't working you know, well that's
her job and that's his job. As long as he is sort of playing
her to do it, paying her all the housekeeping and that, plus
like her extra to do it, I think that's great. I mean it
worked for hundreds and hundreds of years, why not have
a go?

The conceptualization of fairness according to gender was also
mediated by the realities of the market-place. There was an
expectation amongst some, for example – and probably a realistic
one considering the wage differentials of men and women – that
sons were likely to earn more than daughters and, in some cases,
make a greater contribution to the household finances. This point is
taken up later in the discussion of board money. Mr Fox observed,
'Naturally, you expect the boy to earn more than a girl'; and Mrs
McShane, a single parent with four unemployed daughters living
at home, noted not only the disparity in contribution but also
differences in the type of contribution to the household which girls
made:

When me sons were still living here and they were working,
they were all right. But as for the girls, I don't think you
get much money off girls. They help you in the house and
they do their own washing and ironing, keep their rooms
clean and that, but as for getting anything from them,
no.

128

The difference was indeed reflected in the way time was spent by unemployed young people. The young women in the study who were unemployed when interviewed tended to spend more of their time during the day at home than did their male counterparts, and they were much more likely to occupy their time by performing domestic tasks such as cleaning, cooking and child care. For some, however, these heightened gender divisions stemming from a poor labour market were seen as beneficial for future family roles. Some mothers felt that for young women, unemployment at least offered compensation in the chance to acquire domestic skills. Mrs Harris thus commented about her unemployed daughter:

> She'd be able to make a good housewife 'cos she's had plenty of practice. We've got a daughter-in-law going to have a baby soon so they'll be calling on her to help, I expect. Somebody'll have to mind the three children while she's in hospital. I wouldn't mind 'cos at least she's doing something useful.

FAIRNESS AND GENERATION

The notion of fairness entered family life in other ways, affecting relationships between the older and younger generations and amongst siblings. As noted in chapter three, however, a sense of what was fair was also mediated by employment status; workers had certain rights and claims.

Parents constantly attempted to shield their young from feelings of resentment and inadequacy without generating a sense of unfairness, but they interpreted fairness according to particular family cultures. This was illustrated by the negotiations and expectations about young people's contributions towards household expenses. In some families the ideal of fairness was sustained by a flat-rate system, and all the children of working age who had left school paid the same amount of board money irrespective of the source or size of their income. One mother spelled out her reasoning by claiming that as both children received the same household goods and services, so their payments should also be the same. In other cases fairness was incorporated in a system of relativities. Graduated rates were paid according to the size of a young person's income or what parents perceived as young people's needs. Mrs Young, recounting arrangements in her family, explained, 'Bobby was on the lowest wage, he gave the lowest and Stuart got the most, and then Richard got the most when he was working at Mallinson's and so his went up.'

Young people who were saving up to marry were also allowed to contribute less board money than their earnings would seem to merit. There were further hints of the philosophy 'from each according to his ability, to each according to his needs'. Working brothers and sisters would sometimes attempt to mitigate material differences between their own circumstances (Corrigan 1989) and those of an unemployed brother or sister. Borrowing clothes may occur among siblings in normal circumstances, but in this study it was also explicitly seen as a way of helping. Brothers and sisters might give an unemployed sibling money, an act which was reciprocated if the situation were reversed:

> When Kathleen wasn't working, the youngest boy, he only comes in with £30, he used to give her £2 pocket money, you know. But mind when she was working and he was on a YOP scheme, she used to give him a treat, she used to give him a pound or two.

> (Mrs McGuinness)

In some cases parents who could afford it tried to respond to what seemed to them unfair burdens being forced upon young people by giving their unemployed or low-paid children spending money or gifts. Mrs Jones' comments illustrate the importance of a family's economic resources in this respect, and indeed her sacrifice. She admired her son for staying in his job although he was bringing home less than £40 a week, and she helped him out by asking him for only £7-a-week board:

> He gets about £14 back, he doesn't get a very big wage. I suppose some lads pay their mothers an awful lot more, but as they don't get a big wage I don't believe in taking a lot off them. They have to go out and have a bit leisure time and it all takes money so I don't mind as long as I can keep working.

It was clear that transfers were not solely from parent to child. As in Leonard's (1980) study of courtship and marriage, mutual exchanges or reciprocities were involved, not necessarily in equivalent forms. Mr Rice's comment highlights the exchanges in love and material resources taking place in his family:

> There was no way we were gonna see him beat. It's bad

enough being out of work without saying, 'Oh no, I cannot go out at all.' I mean to say we get it back in kind off them – not money-wise, you get it back in other ways off them, because they're as kind to us as what we are to them.

Some attempts to mitigate a young person's situation could, however, create tensions within the family. The 'prodigal son' effect arising from the different personalities of two boys was clear in Mrs Robson's account. When her employed elder son David, a quiet, reserved boy, was unemployed, he had neither asked for nor received any extra money from his parents; she said, 'He wasn't a one for going out when he was on the dole.' Yet Mrs Robson saw her younger, lively unemployed son, Mike, as needing more money. Of his '£15 a week or so' social security money, he gave her £10 board money but received £5-a-week pocket money from her and 'then his dad would give him a fiver'. In addition to legitimate pocket money, she gave him a further £5. 'I feel a bit guilty giving Mike so I sort of sly it to him. David knows Mike gets it, but I sort of give it him on the sly.' She justified her actions by adding, 'But as I say, I used to buy David cigarettes.' The father in this family also expected David to subsidize his brother. According to their mother, during the first few weeks of his job, David

was slipping Mike a couple of pounds, but that stopped, you know. That causes a bit of aggro here because his dad thinks he should sort of give him a bit of pocket money. David doesn't think he should. He thinks Mike gets enough off us.

This was not so much negotiation of the boundaries of reciprocity but an exploration of the notion of what is fair and just.

In their relations with their parents, children also had a sense of fairness. As has been noted in other studies (for example, Leonard 1980; Cusack and Roll 1985), the children, like their parents, were often aware that what they contributed to the household budget did not cover their costs. Kathy Page, for example, had lowered her job aspirations from hairdresser to shop assistant because she knew her parents could not afford to pay for the equipment she would need:

I mean me dad was working on a little wage and there was a canny few of us in, living here at the time. I suppose I didn't want to upset like and let them fork it out and suffer really.

Her sense of what was fair thereby influenced the direction of her life course.

FAMILISM AND FAIRNESS

Obtaining work was a major theme of the study. Looking at the resources people used to obtain jobs highlighted the key value of familism. Again it could be juxtaposed with the concept of fairness, raising dilemmas and contradictions and producing repercussions for the power relationships within the family.

The disillusionment with the promises held out by the education system was described in earlier chapters: the seeming worthlessness to these young people of the few qualifications most had obtained and the renouncement of expectations of any upward occupational mobility, however modest. The confidence inspired by apparent educational change over recent decades seemed to be destroyed. This view of education constituted a strand in what seemed to be a shift to enforced reliance upon more traditional modes of behaviour in which access to work draws upon ties of kinship and affectivity, now more strongly supplementing bureaucratic procedures. This emerged in young people's and parents' feelings that 'rational' means of access to jobs – that is, selection on the grounds of qualifications and ability, in people's eyes the 'fair' means of obtaining work – were fast disappearing. Although from the evidence in Chapter Two few in this study obtained work in this way, adherence to the view was nonetheless repeatedly summed up in the phrase, 'It's not what you know, it's who you know.'

Even in a buoyant economy access to jobs through personal contact – through immediate family, relatives or friends – has been a feature of some occupations. Freedman's (1969) study of part of the American youth labour marked showed that this was especially so as a means of obtaining a first job, and Ashton and Maguire (n.d.)[5] showed that this increased when obtaining second jobs, suggesting the importance of knowledge and contacts gained through work.

However, as jobs have become scarcer and applicants and potential applicants for each job have multiplied, firms have been forced to place more reliance upon informal modes of recruitment. This practice not only carries advantages for the employer but also helps to sustain the familistic imperative, particularly fierce in a cold economic climate, of looking after one's own. Mr Ryan put it bluntly: 'I live by the law of self-preservation, my charity begins at home. That's the way I look at it, you've got to look after your own first.'

The situation, however, is not without its problems. Those employed in firms where it is possible to 'speak for' others may indeed be advantaged in the benefits they can bestow upon friends and family and in the consequent personal power which accrues to them. For as well as reducing the burden of selection for personnel departments, those who introduce a prospective employee in this way are implicitly taking on the uneasy role of guarantor. Some measure of responsibility for good performance implicitly falls upon the employee introducing the new recruit, especially a young one. This was sometimes offered as a reason for the reluctance of some to speak for anyone at all. Mr Page, a lorry driver who had helped both his friends and his son to find work in the past, indicated how an employer could exploit the situation and highlighted the risk the guarantor took with his own reputation:

> Well the first thing they ask is, 'Is he any good? Is he a decent timekeeper?' Well if they are, if you know them that well, you stand a guarantee for them sort of style. If you weren't too sure of a person . . . well you wouldn't ask for him in. Every bad move they make looks on to you.

Writers on exchange theory (see Bulmer 1986) have noted how trust in a person, essential to the development of mutual exchange, is tested by taking incremental risks. To speak for someone is to take a big risk. As Mr Page says, to stand as someone's guarantor means it is important to know them well. It is also important to have some hold over them. The deepest knowledge, both of personal skills and an individual's trustworthiness, of whether or not they are likely to let you down, and the possibility of sanctioning their behaviour, are usually held of immediate family members. This close knowledge, coupled with a sense of familial duty or obligation, gives familism its power. Mr Bryant was able to describe this distinction. His comments also reveal the strength of a child's emotional capital which comes into play in such circumstances:

You'll pull more for a relative than what you will do for a friend, no matter how close your friendship is with that friend. Before me son was in this job I was trying to get a job for me friend, I couldn't get him one. But when it come to me son I tried without even thinking about it. I must have tried ten times harder than what I tried afore when I sat back later and thought about it.

Distinctions of social distance and obligation could also be made between immediate family and other kin, as Mr Ryan observed:

My cousin once approached us to see if I could get her son in and I told her I couldn't help her at all. As I say, if I was gonna get anybody in it would be me own son, but I couldn't even get him in so I couldn't get her son in neither. I mean if there's a job going I speak for them. I think it's me duty to do so. You've got to look after your own first.

For the guarantor, speaking for a son or daughter had other strengths. These rested upon the power relationships between the generations. Some felt that employers gave credence to a parent's recommendation by virtue of the parent's own work performance. The importance of this for a family's reputation, its cultural capital or credit in the labour market and its influence upon child-rearing were noted in Chapter Three. As Mrs Pearce remarked, 'You know, they say, "Well the father's a good worker, therefore the son *may* be"' (emphasis in original).

If employment is gained in this way, however, a child is put on trust, and more than the child's reputation is at stake. The parent risks his or her good name not only as a judge of character, but also as a parent, since the transmission to children of an understanding of the complexities of the norm of trust, in this case trustworthiness, is a major component of parenting. To be let down by one's own child can thus lead to parental anger at the breakdown of reciprocity when an obligation is not fulfilled. It can also induce a sense of shame and embarrassment at the apparent failure in parenting. Parents therefore risk being both 'let down' and 'shown up'.

With one's own children, however, some precautionary steps can be taken. Parents can, for example, explain at length how important such obligations are and at any sign of a breaking of trust sanctions can be invoked – even though, in the end, the behaviour considered to be appropriate cannot be enforced.

The Hamiltons were a good example of this. Mr Hamilton had recently found labouring work for his son, whose long period of unemployment had coincided with his involvement in several incidents of petty crime for which he had twice been fined in the courts. His mother had been exasperated by what, to her, were his 'stupid, childish pranks' and had emphasized that they must stop now that he was working with his father.

When they learned subsequently that Peter had started seeing his old friends again, had missed two days' work and had been reprimanded by his employers, Mr and Mrs Hamilton reminded Peter of his obligations and made their position clear. Mrs Hamilton said: 'It was causing a lot of friction. My husband was saying, "I'll put you out, you can get out this house." And I was saying, "Well you're starting your old tricks again, back in with them."' She felt she was winning the battle over her son's behaviour, however, until:

> the phone rang and it was half past twelve at night and it was this lad. I heard our Peter say, 'Oh no, no, I cannat, man. I've been took in the office, too much of a risk.' At the finish he came upstairs and I says, 'Where are you going?' He says, 'I'm just going – it'll – I'll not be . . .' Eee, well ah went mad. I said, 'Peter, if you don't go to work tomorrow. . . .' I was so annoyed. But in any case he was back within half an hour, so I thought well he must know in his own heart that it's a bad encouragement for him.

Parental power to spell out and go some way towards enforcing obligations is also shown in the following example. Shortly after getting his son a start at his firm, Mr Bryant learned that Malcolm had been asked by a slightly older friend to join him in his work as a self-employed carpet-fitter. Aware that the friend in question had until recently been unemployed for two years, Mr Bryant's amazed and angry reaction to this plan signalled a deep sense of a broken social norm: 'I had just got him a job. This chap tells him to pack it *in*. "Come into the carpet business with me." I says, "*You do that* . . .!"' (emphasis in original).

The contradiction between independence and familism was raised in Chapter Three. It was noted how, at a stage when with the acquisition of an independent income a young person would normally expect some slackening of parental control, work obtained through a parent incurs a debt; an increased sense of obligation to parents, however reluctant, is imported into the labour market. This reverberates in turn upon the relationships within the private domain of home. Yet as fewer job vacancies enter the formal institutional channels (Jenkins *et al*. 1983), those seeking employment must out of necessity increasingly rely upon personal contact. Despite the limits such constraints may hold for personal autonomy, it is the fortunate who have links with the labour market. Mrs Bryant was sorry for those with no links at all.

In more general ways, familism also conflicted with equity, equality and compassion. In the Newcastle families, familial commitment echoed the amoral familism described by Banfield in which

> one cannot afford the luxury of charity, which is giving others more than their due, or even of justice, which is giving them their due. The world being what it is all those that stand outside of the small circle of the family are at least potential competitors and therefore also potential enemies.
>
> (Banfield 1958: 110–11)

Amongst the Newcastle families, such an extreme position was modified by the competing values which still held a place in their changing world: people felt guilt and pity. Thus in many cases there was a consciousness that even in a contracting labour market securing opportunities for one's own children could be to seek out unfair advantage. 'Aren't we a selfish world now?' said Mrs McGuinness when asked if neighbours had helped her two children in their search for work. 'I think if they'd heard about jobs they would have sort of grabbed them themselves because they've all got families.'

The uncomfortable cultural contradiction in societal values between the imperative of familism and the norm of fairness, implicit in the last quotation, was more clearly expressed when the particularism of familism seemed to override the universalistic criteria inherent in the concept of rational bureaucracy in a modern industrial society. Thus parents who had spoken for their children with some success were anxious to explain that their action had not been the critical factor in securing the job. For example, while Mr Fox acknowledged that his position in the firm had helped to get a job for his son, he later added:

I wasn't really instrumental at all. The fact that I worked there helped to a small degree. But *no*, I wouldn't say that influenced them in any way. It was just that the vacancies came up and he was unemployed at the time, so I said to him, 'Look, there's nothing to lose lad. I'll get you an application form and we'll fill it in and see where we go from there.' He was treated as an outside person, there was no favouritism shown towards him because I was already employed there (emphasis in original).

And Mr Hamilton stressed that although he had 'pestered the life out of the personnel officer' on his son's behalf, his son had had a proper interview for the post. On the general question of speaking for, he observed:

Now I'm not absolutely a hundred per cent in favour of this mind, although I did get my own son a job. I think a job should be handled out on *merit*. *Merit*. The job should go to the best man for the job (emphasis in original).

There was also an awareness that when the option lies between doing something for your own child or for another in greater need, familial obligation contravenes the principles not only of equity and equality but also of compassion. Mrs Robson pointed to this:

Well I think everybody's got to look after theirself, you know. Mike's friend, he's nearly 19, he's still not working. I mean we feel sorry for him from a family with no one in work, and Mike's dad says to him, 'I'll try and get you a start next but I had to look after Mike first.' Which you've got to, look after your own.

At the same time there was an acceptance of the limits, in our society, to which family obligations can go. Mrs Pearce acknowledged this when she commented on the response of her uncle who was unable to help her son:

I phoned him a few times but as he said, 'Well I can't. In fact today you phoned me up, tomorrow I've got to go into work and decide about forty who we've got to finish. So,' he says, 'I can't very well finish forty people and then take on a nephew.'

Following her telephone calls for help, Mrs Pearce invited this uncle to her son's engagement party. She had not seen him for six years, 'because they don't mix with the family much'. To her surprise, the invitation was accepted. The incident is rich in suggestion. In times of stress dormant kinship ties may be activated. Even if help cannot be offered, the result, in this case, was to reaffirm familistic bonds of obligation. Because the uncle was unable to provide aid, he possibly felt obliged to demonstrate his commitment to his family. In turn this sustained relationships conducive to future exchanges between family members.

Finally, whilst the imperative of familism seemed to be undermining such important values as equity and independence and denoting a shift towards traditionalism, the traditional value of familism was also under stress by the imperative of seeking work. Earlier chapters showed how lack of local employment could, for example, split up families, with some members leaving for jobs in other parts of the country or abroad and some because of the tensions unemployment caused. Where families remained together, unemployment could lead to stressed relationships within the household.

Moreover, whilst the situation could extend parental power, parental authority and resources could be undermined. The discrepancy between the promise education had held out and the inability of even some highly qualified young people to obtain work raised questions about the value of parental advice and about parents' knowledge of the world. Young people's experience in the changing labour market made certain aspects of parenting redundant, denoting a sea change in industrial time which influenced the ordering of family relationships.

CONCLUSION

The changes in people's lives wrought by a restructuring labour market, chronic anxiety about retaining and obtaining jobs and, in some families, the constantly changing employment statuses of family members, exposed highly regarded values in the culture. This chapter focused on the notions of social contact, reciprocity and trust, and equity, equality and familism to show some of the ways by which families attempt to mediate social change and to suggest how processes within the family, set in train by forces outside it, rebound upon the wider social environment. Members of families are, after all, members of that wider society by virtue of their other statuses and roles as workers, consumers, voters, friends and so forth; but in this case it is aspects of familial roles which penetrate the public domain.

A society's values do not form a unitary system. Thus whilst economic and technical change threatened such deeply held values as the work ethic, it also revealed contradictions within the value system itself. Some of these appeared as contradictions within the same values; others emerged as contradictions posed by competing values. In these situations people had to make uncomfortable and sometimes distressing choices between moral claims.

The economic changes affected power relationships – in the labour market, between men and women and within the family. The Newcastle families were aware of changes in the balance of power between employer and employee and in labour market norms. This is not to say that previously such norms were models of equity, but in the continuous and latent negotiation which goes on between interest groups, and indeed in any social relationship, new and harsher patterns were emerging. In this bargaining both employers and the State were attacking the boundaries of what people felt to be fair and right. This sense of unfairness was expressed in the description of working conditions, poor wages, disillusionment with government schemes for young people and the failure of a society to structure its economy in such a way to give the young opportunities to follow what was seen as a 'normal' pattern of life.

The situation also brought to the fore ambiguities and dilemmas regarding the interrelated themes of individualism and equality, the domestic division of labour and the economic roles of men and women. The economic considerations which a poor labour market forced upon people reinstated underlying social categories such as gender, which could be submerged, although not forgotten, when competition for jobs was less severe.

There were attempts to sustain the practice of fairness in family life. When parents could so afford, they tried to mitigate unemployment for the individual concerned by enhancing subsidies; the young person's contribution to the household economy was regulated by systems (not all the same) which were seen as fair; and, depending how justified the need was seen to be, siblings came to each others' aid as circumstances permitted. As described in Chapter Three, however, work statuses could be a powerful resource in any debate as to what constituted justice. Fairness, also, seemed to work both ways; for children tried to alleviate parents' circumstances.

Families attempted to mediate the situation in several ways. Whilst some began, however reluctantly, to accept unemployment as part of life – at least in the short term – many tried to maintain the status quo. Some parents, for example, tried to ensure that their children were duly treated by their employers, although in such a competitive labour market they were effectively powerless to help. Many adopted strategies to stem the erosion of the work ethic. The bonds of commitment and association (Goffman 1968) that bind people, through obligation and sense of social identity, to the social entities of work and its place in the individual's life were threatened by the chronic lack of jobs and the inadequacies of those that were available. There was consequently a fear amongst some parents that the orientation towards work that they had nurtured would atrophy, leaving their children content not to work but to lead lives dependent upon state benefits. This led to tensions arising from two strands of parenting: love and comfort versus the need to urge young people to retain a desire for work. It led to irritability and family rows, and in some cases, young people left home. Another defence against the threatened erosion of the value of work was, paradoxically, to displace the cause of unemployment from structural problems to those of personal inadequacy. The shame and embarrassment some felt in the presence of unemployment or when unemployed suggested the strategies of avoidance Douglas (1975) refers to as evidence of attacks on a society's beliefs.

Familism itself proved to be an ideological resource in meeting problems, but it was also a source of moral dilemmas and contradiction. Thus the use of a parent's social capital, vested in influence over access to jobs, could sometimes achieve a place in the work-force for a child. This, however, highlighted a contradiction within familism itself, since enhanced familial power was conveyed into the workplace when one of the tenets of good parenting was the encouragement of independence. This was related to a further dilemma. The imperative of the particularistic value of familism in our society – ensuring that parents give their own children priority over the claims of others – created a sense of unease. It overrode the universalistic norm of fairness whereby, in the competition for jobs, all are treated according to merit. There was a hint of a movement towards a more traditional and selfish society in which each family looked after its own, keeping close rather than sharing knowledge which might provide entry into the labour force.

Finally, there was the stress placed on the family and familism itself when a job search took children away from the parental home, causing distress for some parents and children, or when emotional and economic tensions caused young people to leave home, as they in some cases did.

6

CONCLUSION

This book has been about social change in the lives of forty ordinary working-class families in the urban North-East of England. In one sense, therefore, it is both limited and parochial: limited in the range of views and experiences to which members of forty families can give voice, parochial in its regional location, particularly the North-East with its endemic high rates of unemployment which, it is sometimes argued, render this region different from other parts of the country. In another sense, however, it speaks for a much wider population. The impact of technological and economic change, particularly in the effect upon labour markets, has been felt throughout British society. Although patterns and responses may vary according to differences in social class, region and labour market, the book has shown that the anxieties, fears and behaviours which flow from a poor labour market and which are particularly evident in families where young members are without jobs are also found in families apparently untouched by unemployment. This suggests that changing labour markets impinge upon the lives of people far beyond those immediately affected. The book shows how widely and deeply those tentacles reach – into society, into the family and into the individual.

In all lives the changes of biography and history intersect. The book has focused on how a changing and restructuring local labour market and the changes associated with that transitional stage between the dependency of childhood and full adulthood intersect in the context of family life. It has looked at the mediation of this intersection through the interaction of family members in the routines of family life, and at the effect upon the expectations and ordering through which people try to make sense of their existence. The chapters take up the theme of these intersecting

142

changes in different ways – in the labour market experience itself and the uncertainties that were produced, in the young person's struggle towards independence within the family, in the effect of change upon the construction of the social order by which we try to give shape and meaning to our lives and gain a sense of fit, and in the contradictions and prioritizing of values which change brings to the fore.

Change exposes power. The ambience of change in which people in the study lived reflected their powerlessness especially the kaleidoscopic changes in the employment status of family members, the way families drew upon their resources to help their young into the labour market and the realization that some of these resources were now devalued, inappropriate or lost because of the changes in the labour market itself. The search for work, and experiences in work, suggested a shift in power between employer and employee and a restatement of labour market norms in a harsher economic climate. This was described in Chapter Two.

The poor labour market also penetrated the power relationships within the family and, in some cases, extended parental power into the world of work. Chapter Three explored the role of the high moral status and power of paid employment in young people's negotiation for independence, highlighting the relationships between the generations and amongst siblings. For parents and children the renegotiation of the boundaries of control was not, however, a practice which suddenly emerged as an issue when the young person left school and entered the world of work. Independence was not only bound to expectations and an image of the future, the promise of economic independence from waged work and a separate domestic life; it was also rooted in a familistic past deeply informed with elements of the work ethic, the imperative of paid employment, the value and moralities of time and money, the reliability of the good worker and self-reliance. Disruption to life-course expectations when young people were denied the economic and social resources provided by paid employment led to stress, tension and bewilderment; with so few jobs available, and the movement between unemployment and government schemes over the passing years, some become resigned to this condition.

The poor labour market meant that parental power, usually confined to the private domain of the family, could enter the public domain of work if parents were able to find jobs for their children. This produced obligations on the part of the young person and responsibility for good performance on the part of the parent. Change in the labour market was echoed by reported fluctuations in maturity as young people moved in and out of work, and status and negotiating power for use with siblings as well as parents was clearly tied to work status.

The effects of a poor labour market entered family life in more intimate ways. This was explored through the concept of time. For unemployed young people and those in temporary, low-paid, and insecure jobs, futures were uncertain. But those who were unemployed were also thrust outside those patterns and routines of the everyday world which foster belonging. They not only lacked an externally imposed structure to their day but were in the way of those who had to conform to such structures. They became displaced from family discourse and felt they had little to contribute to family talk after the end of the working day. They became sensitive to teasing and banter. Descriptions of their condition and the language used to express it revealed the subservient status and lower order of citizenship to which they felt they had been consigned and which was reflected in others' behaviour towards them. The structures of time, work and money not only produced a moral order from which they were excluded but also one which their condition challenged. Thus unemployment posed a threat to the way some perceived the proper order to the world, creating embarrassment and a tendency to blame the individual.

Change also exposed contradictions in the culture. Thus in addition to the material and emotional uncertainty of their lives, people had to cope with the ambiguities in cultural values. Even if regretfully, people had to look first to their own survival. The universalistic norm of equity and fairness was, it seemed, more obviously giving way to the particularistic norm of familism. When jobs were scarce, families had to look after their own. The unease created was clear in the length at which some people explained either how they disagreed with the practice of speaking for but had been forced into this by circumstances, or how all applicants had been subject to formal selection procedures. Gender also became an issue, challenging the ideal of equality in views about who had most need of a job when future family responsibilities were taken into account.

There was also a realization that it is possible to carve out an existence, even if inadequately, in ways which contradicted a sense of what was proper or, indeed, legal, and, by some, a querying of the rules themselves. Some parents feared that their children might be forced into an existence on social security, grow accustomed to it, and lose the urge for work. Families attempted to sustain the pattern and values of their family life against the inroads which societal change was making into their private world. They drew upon time, money, patience, authority, contacts and knowledge in their attempts to support their young. They consciously tried to sustain notions of fairness between siblings, although work status could hold sway here. Attempts were made to mediate tensions, particularly by mothers. They did what they could. They had to prepare their children for a changing world whilst attempting to sustain those beliefs and practices they valued.

Baier (1985) argues that society gives parents the role of socializing the young into the moral community, and that such a community is premised upon the notion of trust. Underlying the detail here, however, was a sense that young people had been let down – by society in general and by state and government in particular. An implicit bargain was being defaulted upon. Those young people who might never hold a job were consigned to a second order of citizenship, unable to join or contribute to the community. The experience of the Newcastle families suggests that notions of trust and reciprocity remained an important strand in family life, but families were living in a broader climate in which the various kinds of trust on which relationships were founded were undergoing change. This is not to say that this dimension of relationships should or can remain static, nor that the world owes young people a living. There was, however, a profound sense that a modern wealthy society owes more to its younger members, and that with political will this could be achieved.

Since the completion of this study economic and political change has swept across Eastern and Western Europe, exposing the fragility and interconnectedness of social order in public and private domains. Although this will vary across cultures (Allatt 1990), what such changes herald, and indeed are about, are the destruction, creation and redistribution of resources out of which both societies and individuals create social order. For many people, because of the major areas of life which it underpins, the foremost of these resources is income from paid employment. The place of the young in the new economic order remains uncertain; but the power of the economic to penetrate the remote corners of social existence means that, even in supportive families, those without this resource are in danger of being socially dislodged and disconnected from both large and small social units which constitute a society.

APPENDICES

APPENDIX 1: ELDON: BACKGROUND INFORMATION ABOUT THE AREA

'Eldon', the ward in Newcastle upon Tyne where the study was conducted, contains some 4,300 households and a population of approximately 11,000 people. This appendix provides information about the area's housing, amenities, employment, political complexion and social problems at the time of the study.

HOUSING

Most of the housing within the ward was built in the inter-war period. There is a variety of accommodation, about 90 per cent of which belongs to the local authority. This includes conventional housing estates, deck-access dwellings, and some multi-storey accommodation. The area is acknowledged as one needing substantial resources for housing improvement schemes, and these are gradually being made available (City of Newcastle upon Tyne 1981a). Nevertheless, officers of the city council expressed the view that basic housing rights were being denied within the ward in some cases, noting that certain properties lacked one or more of the following: an adequate heating system; an adequate kitchen; sound windows; sound roof; damp-free floors.

The area includes some pockets of 'junk housing', which are used to absorb any potential problems of homelessness. Such property includes some blocks of housing, first occupied in 1969, which suffered from water penetration problems due to a flat roof design and which were later designated as unsuitable for families with children. Although some improvements had been carried out

147

here, lettings difficulties and continued deterioration had led to a decision to demolish the blocks and replace them with low-rise developments. One of the young men studied was living in such a block, awaiting rehousing, when he was interviewed. A further block of five-storey accommodation just outside the Eldon boundary had been converted into 200 units for single persons. It was not popular with tenants and had an inadequate heating system, but was nevertheless accessible to young people. In April 1983 about forty of the 200 units were unoccupied. Council officers remarked that the accommodation was 'not really suitable' for young people, commenting that they were mixing there with 'winos and the mentally ill', that the place was 'unsupervised' with 'no social control' and had a reputation for solvent abuse problems. It was nevertheless a possible source of accommodation for young people seeking to live independently of their families, and some of the informants were offered accommodation there. Improvements planned for this block included controlled entries and improvements to the heating system.

Sales of local authority housing had been taking place, although when the study commenced only the best housing stock – the three-bedroomed, centrally heated properties – were affected. The maximum value on such a property in Eldon was then about £16,000; all eligible tenants qualified for a 33 per cent reduction on this value, and some for a 50 per cent reduction. They were also entitled to a council mortgage. Officers of the council estimated the replacement cost of such a house at £23,000.

Overcrowding continues to be a problem in the area, and the 1981 census showed that 8 per cent of households suffered from overcrowding (using a definition of more than one person per room). The estimated figure (due to changes in ward boundaries) for the same area in 1971 was 15.6 per cent.

In an attempt to improve services to tenants, the council set up a housing management scheme in the area in 1983. This involved the establishment of five project offices within the housing area, two of which were within the Eldon ward boundary. It was hoped that this would lead to a more effective housing maintenance service, better able to respond quickly to local needs. The ward contains several tenants' associations, which seek to further the interests of tenants living in particular local areas within the ward. At least one of these concerned itself with youth and community issues in addition to housing matters.

148

AMENITIES

Leisure and sports

The ward contains two parks, one of which has a staffed adventure playground, tennis courts and a bowling green. Further improvements were planned at this site and a competition for ideas about how it should be developed had been run in 1983. This park was affected by some vandalism problems. The other park was the product of a mid-1960s reclamation scheme but, partly as a result of drowning incidents early on, had never been a great success. Improvements planned at the outset of the study included the building of a motor-cycle track and of a workshop where young people could do bike repairs, etc.

The local sports centre was built in the mid-1960s and required substantial upgrading. Under a partnership scheme, various improvements were planned, including building a swimming pool, improving the running track, and building a new gymnasium, exercise room and sauna. Work began on these during the course of the study.

The swimming baths serving the area were very old, with substandard changing facilities. Just before the study commenced the opening hours had been altered and the charging system changed in an attempt to promote use of these baths.

There were two main youth clubs and several small ones in the Eldon area. One of the former provided us with an interviewing room which was used when young people preferred not to be interviewed at home. Free daytime leisure activities for unemployed people (who did not need to be club members) were run by the main clubs. One club reported use of this facility by about twenty-five young people, mostly young men.

One of the local churches had a community centre which was developing its activities, with funding from the city council, and expanding its range of services for local people during the period of the research. Developments included a youth workshop and the provision of opportunities for various recreation and learning skills, following some local research into the needs of unemployed people in the ward.

Welfare and health

The Eldon resource centre was providing a one-to-one advice service about welfare rights, fuel debt problems, etc., and also a base for the Eldon leisure project worker whose brief was to respond to demand for resources of various kinds for leisure provision within the area. At the time of the study the centre had six Community Programme/Community Enterprise Programme-funded workers – two each for photography, sports, and a video project. The Resource Centre was trying to reach more local people and to inform them of local activities by widespread leafletting. This centre also housed a health project with a worker. In addition, welfare rights sessions were run in a vacant shop in the Eldon shopping centre.

Eldon contains two health centres, but council officials expressed the view that there were probably inadequate numbers of GPs serving the ward. There was also a shortage of local chemists' shops.

Transport

According to the 1981 census, 81.6 per cent of households in Eldon are without the use of a car or van. This compares with an estimated figure of 84.1 per cent in 1971. There is thus great reliance on public provision. The ward does not contain a train station, but the nearest ones (in neighbouring wards) are used by Eldon residents. Two main bus routes serve Eldon, both providing access to the city centre.

Shops

The main shopping area in Eldon contains two (small) super-markets, but the area is otherwise poorly served. The co-op supermarket closed recently, and five shops in another part of the ward were demolished. There are few corner shops, and shopping is known to be a problem in Eldon, especially for the elderly. The nearest main shopping area outside the ward is some two miles from the centre of Eldon. Council officers observed that whilst facilities were inadequate for the needs of local people, it was unlikely that many more shops could be run within the area as commercially viable concerns.

Educational facilities

Eldon has a public library, which contains a notice-board displaying job centre vacancies. The city council's report 'High unemployment in the inner city' (City of Newcastle upon Tyne 1981) highlighted the importance of this facility for unemployed people, especially in the 25 to 44 age group. According to the report, unemployed people are significantly more likely to use this facility than their employed counterparts.

Children from Eldon attend a variety of schools. Several primary schools and the Eldon comprehensive school are situated within the ward, while some local children of secondary-school age attend schools outside the ward, especially one Roman Catholic comprehensive school which lies well outside the ward boundary.

EMPLOYMENT

Employment opportunities in the local area have declined rapidly in recent years. By 1981, the male unemployment rate (men aged 16–64) had risen to 29.6 per cent (from 16.0 per cent in 1978), and 12.5 per cent of economically active women (aged 16–59) were unemployed. These figures for Eldon are markedly worse than those for the larger area of Newcastle upon Tyne in which it is situated.

In general terms, the decline in shipbuilding and heavy engineering has had severe effects on male employment. Despite this, however, one local heavy engineering firm remains a major employer in the area, although its work-force of thousands is greatly reduced from its former strength. What remains of the shipbuilding and ancillary industries in Newcastle upon Tyne is local to the area where the study was conducted, but this industry draws labour from throughout the city and nearby Wallsend, and has not served to cushion the local population in Eldon from the redundancies and unemployment which are now endemic to the area.

Other local employers include a food-processing plant and offices of the Department of Health and Social Security (DHSS; now the Department of Social Security, DSS) both of which are located outside the Eldon area but provide some employment for Eldon residents.

POLITICS

At the parliamentary level, Eldon is contained within one of the Newcastle constituencies. Its Member of Parliament (SDP-Labour until March 1982) lost his seat to the Labour candidate in the May 1983 general election. All the local councillors are Labour. However, despite the strong hold which the Labour party has in both local electoral and parliamentary terms, active party involvement at grass-roots level is unusual. Green (1981) records the constituency Labour party as having only 300 members in 1977, and estimates party membership in the area as a whole at a ratio of 1:122 of the electorate at that date.

The efforts of local councillors on behalf of the Eldon area have yielded the allocation of some of the city's available funds for improvements and projects. Housing resources allocated to the area have already been mentioned. In addition, the city council's estimate that within the city Eldon ranks near the bottom on its social and economic deprivation criteria, together with its policy of positive discrimination and the efforts of local councillors, have ensured that Eldon gets a good share of other available resources. Funds have been made available under the Inner City Partnership Scheme, and Eldon is designated a priority area. The priority area team had a budget of £50,000 per annum in 1983, and the Eldon Leisure Project was funded with £60,000 from Partnership funds. Other local amenities and projects funded by the city council include youth clubs, the resource centre, the community health project, etc.

SOCIAL PROBLEMS

In addition to the problems associated with unemployment, poor housing and the inadequate supply of certain amenities, two other problems – fuel debt and crime – need to be mentioned here.

Fuel debt

The cost of heating the home was identified as a significant problem in relation to unemployment in the city council's report, 'High unemployment in the inner city' (City of Newcastle upon Tyne 1981b). Although 2 per cent of households in which no one was unemployed had been unable to pay a recent heating bill, this figure rose to 10 per cent in households in which someone, but not the head of household, was out of work, and to 23 per cent and 18 per cent respectively where the head of household was unemployed, short term and long term. Many more households in this study reported that they were experiencing difficulties in paying such bills: in households in which the head of household was employed but which contained at least one unemployed person, this figure rose to 31 per cent. The Newcastle upon Tyne Energy Advice Unit was set up in 1979 on the initiative of the city council. At the outset of the study, a worker there observed that a marked increase in fuel debt problems had been noted over the previous 18 months. The unit had a worker in the Eldon welfare rights office whose brief was to provide a debt counselling service in Eldon. A domestic heating advice project was also being established in Eldon. This was to have four staff in posts funded by the Manpower Services Commission's Community Programme.

Crime

Crime, particularly of a petty nature, causes considerable problems within the ward. Car theft and theft from cars, petty burglary and housebreaking and other types of juvenile crime are all recognized as local problems, and certain small areas within Eldon are known to be badly affected.

APPENDIX 2: RESEARCH DESIGN

TYPE OF RESEARCH

The type of research adopted and the methods used for data collection were guided by the paucity of knowledge on youth unemployment and family relations. An inductive exploratory design was chosen which would allow the researchers to assume as little as possible, include as much information as could be managed, and allow people to develop accounts of their experiences in their own way (see Piotrkowski 1979 for a detailed discussion of this type of research). The need was to uncover key themes and complex processes. Consequently, a detailed qualitative study of two small matched groups of families varying only on the employment status of the young person (designated as the 'focal informant') was deemed more appropriate than a large-scale survey. The latter would have provided tighter questions for comparison and analysis, but less opportunity for discursive responses and exploratory probing.

It would, moreover, have been premature, if not impossible, to study the relative frequency of some fact or attempt to test causal relationships between known and measurable variables. Like Komarovsky's (1962) study, the aim here was to capture the patterns of the relationships and reactions of family members as established ways and values were challenged by high rates of youth unemployment. Such an exercise could not only lay out at least some of the groundwork for future studies but also, by assuming that people are not unique, generate theoretical (as opposed to statistical) generalizations and significant descriptions about complex processes and relationships (Piotrkowski 1979).

LOCATION

Not only, therefore, was there to be no attempt to generalize from the study in any statistical sense, but neither was a community study envisaged. Informants, however, must live somewhere, and by locating them within the same, small neighbourhood some of the variation between families could be reduced.

The advantages in selecting Eldon ward were twofold. First, work on local labour markets in Newcastle (Cousins 1980) showed that Eldon was a more self-contained and stable ward with regard to population movements than elsewhere in Newcastle. In particular, adult children were more likely to live in the same ward as parents. Second, preliminary discussions with local government officials, teachers, youth workers and the police, some of whom had grown up in the area, suggested that this was a neighbourhood which over many years had been held in high regard by local people. Eldon was seen as a predominantly respectable working-class community with a strong work ethic[1] (see Appendix One for a detailed description of the neighbourhood). This was of theoretical importance because of the study's focus upon ordinary families rather than those who were particularly poor or otherwise disadvantaged. Following entry into the field some accommodation was made in this respect. This is discussed below.

DEVELOPMENT OF THE RESEARCH DESIGN

Shifts and changes in the economy and labour market not only had important implications for people's lives but underlay the methodological difficulties which arose in the selection of families on which the effects of such changes could be studied. The details of the selection process are noted in Appendix Three. Here, because social change lies at the heart of the study, it is important briefly to describe the development of the research design. By taking cognizance of the real world and embracing its complexities (rather than merely recognizing them and the limitations that they may impose upon any subsequent findings) it was possible, in this case, more tightly to integrate theory, method and the real world. What took place was a move from what Brown and Kidwell (1982: 833) described as 'obligatory genuflexions to the dictums of good research' to that which Campbell and Stanley (1963: 71) have called 'the possibility of creatively using the idiosyncratic features of any specific research situation in designing unique tests of [in their case] causal hypothesis'. In doing this the efficiency of the sample design was increased, first by cutting costs, both financial and emotional; second, in becoming a tool of greater heuristic value; and third, in advancing the analysis even prior to the collection of the data.

In this study the principal design difficulties were linked. The first was that of comparison: against what criteria were any findings on the unemployed informants and their families to be assessed? The second was the number of variables which might impinge upon family relationships. These were not extraneous variables but were inherent to the subject matter of the study. Employment statuses, for example, could not only include permanent, temporary, full-time, part-time and intermittent employment as well as unemployment, but, in the present economic climate, employment statuses were also fragile and could change during the course of the contact with a family, as indeed some did.

There is a substantial body of research, including some on unemployment (Komarovsky 1971; McKee and Bell 1986; Pilgrim Trust 1938), which does not include a control group for comparison. While criticized by some (Campbell and Stanley 1963), such studies are important in contributing to that wealth of empirical data essential for the construction of hypotheses worth testing (Stacey 1969). The location of the present study in the North-East, however – with its historically high level of unemployment relative to other parts of the country – made the inclusion of a control group crucial. To confine the study to the unemployed would mean that any observations could as easily be attributed to the characteristics of the region as to the effects of the recent recession. Thus, despite the precedent in the literature, for comparative purposes the ideal design would incorporate two groups of families, those of employed and those of unemployed young people.

A non-probability sample was chosen, with two groups of families which were to differ only on the criterion of the selected young person's (focal informant's) employment status. The mother, father and the focal informant were to be interviewed (see Appendix Three) and the two groups were to be matched on the major variables of age, gender and education of the focal informants; attempts were also to be made to match rather than screen out other important variables. These included the employment status of parents, family size, number of siblings and the employment status of siblings. The difficulty of this task was recognized but, as in many studies of this kind, it was felt that the complexity would enrich the quality of the findings in an area where the issues were so unexplored.

This was prophetic. To match families on the age, sex and education of the focal informant was straightforward, but the additional variables of employment statuses of household members, especially when combined with family size, raised severe problems. For this study numbers were necessarily small because of the time-consuming nature of qualitative research and the amount of data it generates; but the sampling frame of 240 (the list of young people of the selected age group held by the careers office), although apparently sizeable, proved too small to produce sufficient families for matching. Even confining attention to employment statuses, the pilot study and the household screening revealed such variation within and between families that the matched sample of standard experimental design could have no heuristic value. Other researchers on unemployment have also met this problem; their funding body eventually withdrew the requirement for a matched sample and the research was confined to the unemployed group (Bell and McKee 1982). But, as already noted, in the present case these confounding variables were so intimately related to the purpose of the study that they could not be so disregarded. The effect of a young person's unemployment on a family is intricately bound up with the employment statuses of other family members.

Furthermore, variation of employment statuses within a family, and changes in these statuses, could serve to make visible in family life those patterns and values normally latent. In sum, complexity and flux were the essence of the situation in which these families found themselves. To screen this out, or rather ignore it, given that matching was impracticable, would have seriously misrepresented or grossly oversimplified the real world of people's experiences and lives, and limited the value of any findings.

It was by turning, in desperation, to the construction of a typology of all the relevant variables, and starting with the typology of employment statuses and family composition, that the basis of the comparison was redesigned. The two components to the comparison remained but in a different form. There was now to be a core group of two-parent families in which all members in the economically active age group (those between the ages of 16 and retirement age who are able to work) fulfilled the heretofore work expectations of our society – that is, they were in full-time employment or full-time education, with the exception of the mother. The mother could be either in paid employment or a homemaker by choice, as neither status contravenes the usual expectations of our society. Against this 'core' or 'standard' or 'normal' group was to be set the complexity of situation and response in families where a member or members had experienced unemployment, whether past or present. Thus at a time when normative expectations were threatened, the impact of unemployment could, it was felt, be assessed against a normative group which had apparently suffered little or no change. The theoretical basis of the study was now firmly incorporated into a method of investigation more firmly aligned with the real world.

The design also allowed for a more efficient use of resources by allowing the inclusion of co-operative families who would previously have been excluded either because of employment patterns or because of their different family types – for example, single-parent families. More importantly (although not taken up in this book), there was now the potential for investigating not only the impact of unemployment upon those families considered to be 'ordinary' or 'normal' but also, because they could be examined against this core group of two-parent families, those already designated (correctly or incorrectly) as vulnerable – single parent families or the families of those with unemployed parents – could also be included in the investigation. A further advantage was that this design provided a stronger methodological base for any future comparative work. It was, in fact, only by having such a control group that the impact of the uncertainties in the labour market – not only upon the unemployed, but also upon families who were apparently unaffected by unemployment – could be recognized.

ANALYSIS

The analysis was derived from themes which emerged from the data. A view of culture as embracing a plurality of emphases rather than distinct differences (Thompson 1984) has methodological implications for the extraction of themes and how they are used in the analysis. Thus, in this view an item that occurs once is as important to the analysis and the interpretation, and is given as much weight, as one that occurs many times. This is because each is seen as a strand in a total cultural configuration. While further investigation and analysis (even of the same data) would add to the understanding of the complexities of this configuration and realign and modify the constituent elements, knowledge provided by the present study would remain an intrinsic part of the whole. Representativeness, therefore, is not present in any statistical sense – that is, how widespread or how frequently these themes occur; rather, that which is uncovered in this study represents an important aspect of our culture because of the fact that it occurs at all (Murcott 1983).

It will be evident, from this, that the analysis was firmly grounded in the data; the themes were not imposed but were present in and emerged from people's responses. The higher order categories and concepts into which these elements could be grouped had the strength both of being recognizable to people themselves – for example, the concept of fairness – in their daily lives, and of having theoretical echoes in the literature (see Glaser and Strauss 1967). It was this which gave the analysis its particular excitement.

APPENDIX 3: FINDING THE FAMILIES: STUDY GROUP AND INTERVIEWS

The names of all 1980–81 school-leavers living in Eldon ward and born before 1 September 1965 were extracted from the computerized lists held by Newcastle upon Tyne Careers Service and the 'dormant' files of those over 18 who had ceased to register with them. The age of 18 was taken as the lower age, as this meant that the prospective informants would have had at least one year's experience in the labour market, eligibility for the YOP having ceased. This yielded 240 families from which the study group was to be selected.

THE APPROACH

Letters were sent to three members of each of the 240 families (mother, father and young person) – all of whom, it was hoped, would be interviewed – explaining the study and asking for the recipient's permission for the researchers to contact him or her. A returnable slip to refuse permission and a freepost envelope were included. If any member of a family refused at this stage, the entire family was eliminated from the study (92 families). Those not refusing were screened by means of a brief formal interview for details of household composition, current employment statuses of household members, members who had left home, the employment history of the focal informant and any disability in the household. The pilot study had revealed how the latter could dominate a household, unemployment becoming merely an additional burden to that already carried. To isolate the impact of unemployment, families of the disabled were excluded. Suitable times for an interview were noted. These data were then sorted and, for those families which fitted the criteria, arrangements were made for an interview by either telephone or personal visit.

To conserve resources, and in fairness to those concerned, potential informants were told how long the interviews would last and, although the interviewer's approach was consciously positive, people were not persuaded to agree to an interview when unwilling. Even so, a few respondents withdrew at a later stage or failed to keep appointments. The final group comprised 40 families. Of the 200 refusals, 92 were by letter, 16 at the screening stage, 6 at the appointment stage, 40 families were unsuitable and 46 could not be contacted. Tables A3.1 and A3.2 show the numbers, family status and gender of the respondents in the families interviewed. Table A3.3 shows the employment statuses of the focal informants at the time of the first interview. (Some statuses, indeed, had

Table A3.1 Members interviewed in 40 families

No. of family members interviewed	No. of families
4	1
3	18
2	10 (including 3 single-parent families)
1	11 (including 1 orphan)

Table A3.2 Family status and gender of respondents

Family status of respondents	
Mothers	30
Fathers	20
Female focal informants	15
Male focal informants	20
Focal informants' siblings	4
Total respondents	89

Table A3.3 Employment status of 40 young people at the time of first interview

Sex	Employed	Unemployed
Male	12*	11
Female	9	8
Total	22	19

Note: * Includes 1 part-time.

Table A3.4 Family structure at time of first interview

Structure	No. of families
Two-parent family	33
Single-parent family	5
Left a two-parent family	1
Orphan	1
Total	40

changed between this stage and the screening stage.) Table A3.4 shows the family structure of respondents at the time of the first interview.

INTERVIEWING AND SCREENING

The original intention was to integrate screening and interviewing by staggering the dispatch of letters. The purpose was to avoid long intervals between screening and interview during which the family situation could change. The low response rate and the strict criteria for selection made this strategy unworkable, resulting in delay in the interviewing. Thus, after the initial attempt, letters of approach were sent out in larger batches and intensive screening undertaken.

The yield from the first set of screening allowed interviewing to start in September 1983. The last interview took place in November 1984. Data were collected from each of the three family members by means of two tape-recorded interviews held approximately one week apart, during which period informants were asked to keep a diary for a day. Attempts were made to interview each informant alone, although this was not always possible. Length of interview ranged from 45 minutes to $3\frac{1}{2}$ hours, averaging $1\frac{1}{2}$–2 hours. On completion, tapes were transcribed and the transcripts edited and annotated.

Care was taken to pace interviews to allow for annotation, checking of themes covered, amendments to leading questions for future interviews, omissions and promising lines of enquiry to be pursued in the second interview. Burgoyne (1983) has noted the dangers of arranging interviews too closely and the importance of having time for reflection. Approximately five interviews a week could be conducted satisfactorily by an interviewer.

Despite the precautions noted above, it was recognized that one member of a family might refuse an interview after some interviewing in the family had already taken place. Priorities had therefore to be established; where possible the mother, as the member most likely to be aware of the internal dynamics of family relationships, was approached first, followed by the young person or father. Both interviews were completed before arrangements were made to interview the second member of the family. Arrangements were also made for informants to be interviewed outside the home in a local youth club if they preferred. Where possible, two interviewers were involved with each family, and account was taken of the gender of the interviewer and informant.

The interviewing team comprised the two full-time researchers and two part-time interviewers. In addition, a part-time market research interviewer was employed for the household screening.

During the interviewing period, regular meetings were held to alert the interviewing team to any activity in the community or to any new themes or leads emerging in the data, and to weld the interviewers as a team so that diversification of interest, which is a danger in semi-structured interviewing, could be curbed or assimilated where necessary.

The interview schedules covered the following areas for investigation and contained model questions by which topics could be both introduced and probed: labour market and work, networks, domestic division of labour, peer group, authority and control within the family, household day and diary, family resources, education, health, family history, voting.

There were two basic schedules, one for the young person and one for parents. These were adjusted to the situations of employment, unemployment, recent change of employment situation, gender and differences in household composition.

A diary, to be kept for one day, was designed not just as a tool to explore daily routine but primarily to open up discussion about the social contacts and relationships of both informant and family which might have otherwise been difficult to pursue. A diary entry made by the informant legitimated such questioning and collection of the diary also eased entry into the second interview.

APPENDIX 4: YOUNG PEOPLE AND EMPLOYMENT STATUS AT FIRST INTERVIEW

Name	Status[1]	Name	Status[1]
Shirley Hewitt	E	Andrew Black	E
Marie Davis	E	Martin Johnson	E
Karen Hughes	E	Kevin Ryan	U
Kathy Page	U	Malcolm Bryant	E
Dawn Harris	U	David Mitchell	E

Caroline Price	E	Mark Freeman	E
Sandra Cross	U	Gerald Rice	E
Christine Dyer	U	Ian Potter	E
Angela Ward	U	Michael West	U
Carol Knight	U	Philip Thompson	U
Clare Howard	E	Peter Hamilton	E
Kathleen McGuinness	E	Neil Peters	U
Annette Maynard	U	Paul Fox	U
Margaret Hills	E	Geoffrey Lewis	U
Hilary Jenkins	E	Stuart Drake*	U
Joanna McGuire	U	Umar Kahn	U
Cheryl Reynolds	E	Hugh Clark	U
Bryan Jones	E	Stephen Wood	U
Phil Matthews	E	Martin Pearce	E
John Phillips	U	David Robson	E

Note: 1. E = Employed; U = Unemployed.

    *Stuart Drake's mother had remarried – she was now Mrs Kelly.

NOTES

1 INTRODUCTION: FAMILY, HISTORY AND BIOGRAPHY

1. Where the family has been taken into account, for example in advice upon jobs (Rathkey n.d.), this has frequently been tangential to the major research questions about the individual's response, perceptions and expectations, or the role of the formal institutions of education, trade unions, industry and so forth. It would seem that, generally, a traditional field of enquiry for both sociology and psychology has been transposed to the transition from school to non-work (Griffin 1987).

   There are a few exceptions to these approaches. Griffin (1985) and Bates (n.d.a, n.d.b), for example, look at the role of the family in the gendered construction of girls' work identities; Wallace (1987) at the effects of a poor labour market on young people's domestic careers; whilst Hutson and Jenkins (1989) focus upon the relationships themselves between parents and their unemployed adult children in the transition to adulthood.

2. There are two thrusts to the social policy changes affecting young people. One set of changes aims to increase the flexibility of the labour market through the removal of protective legislation governing the pay, hours, rights and conditions of work for young people. These are discussed in this chapter.

   The second set of changes shifts the responsibility for those who need economic support during these years from the state to the family. In some instances control over resources is transferred from the young person to the parents (Bradshaw *et al.* 1987: 18). Moreover, several legal changes extend the deemed age of dependency into the mid-twenties, up to the age of 26 in the 1985 Board and Lodging Regulations.

   The policies are not without their contradictions. Some, such as the changes to the housing benefit regulations described by Cusack and Roll (1985) and the community charge, render the economic cost of young people too much for some families to sustain, whilst others, implicitly and explicitly, force teenagers and young adults back upon the family for support. This is irrespective of whether or not they are welcome or the

164

family can afford to subsidize them, or whether, indeed, there is a home to go to (Allatt 1988a).

Thus the community charge with which the government has replaced the domestic rating system, levies a flat rate charge on all residents of an area aged 18 years and over (except a few living in institutions), with the maximum rebate available for those on low incomes set at 80 per cent. Households containing adult children will often be paying a community charge which is higher than the rates it replaces. Meanwhile, since the 1987 Social Security Act, single childless persons under 25 years old will receive reduced rates of Income Support. In the paper which preceded the Act the government stated,

> It is clear that at the age of 18 the majority of claimants are not fully dependent and that the majority of claimants above the age of 25 are. . . . The government have concluded that an appropriate dividing line is age 25.
> (Social Security Act 1987, Cmnd. 9518 II para 2.73, quoted in Youthaid 1986a:4)

Harris' (1988) useful survey of the policy changes since 1980 which affect young people's independence includes the following not already mentioned: the raising of the minimum age of entitlement to Income Support from 16 to 18 (Social Security Act 1988); the removal from the young unemployed in 1984, for those under 21 and later for those aged 21–24, of the eligibility for the non-householder's contribution towards household costs – £3 per week which a non-householder might reasonably be expected to contribute towards the householder's expenses; and reductions in students' housing, unemployment and supplementary benefit entitlements, (including the removal of short-vacation entitlement to unemployment benefit and supplementary benefit, thereby increasing dependence on parents).

3. A study in South Wales of 18–25-year-olds and their parents, which focused on 'the interactional complexities of family life' (Hutson and Jenkins 1987: 38; 1989), started in 1985, in the final phases of the Newcastle study.

4. In February 1989, noting the drop in unemployment to below two million, *The Economist* (1989) estimated that about a quarter of the reduction in recorded unemployment over the last three years was due to new methods of accounting, and that 'not all of the rest is attributed to unemployed people taking jobs', since the nature of the jobs, many part-time, is attracting women into the labour force. The Unemployment Unit and Youthaid (1989) estimate the actual levels of unemployment to be throughout the UK: 8.8 per cent (6.1); Northern Region: 13.4 per cent (9.2); South-East: 5.5 per cent (3.8) (unadjusted figures; official figures in brackets). Since 1979 there have been more than twenty changes in the methods of accounting. The following are some of the major ones which have contributed to the reductions in the official records of unemployment:

–After October 1982 the system of counting the unemployed changed from registration to claimants.

165

–From April 1983 the provisions of the budget mean that some aged 60 and over no longer sign on at an employment office.

–Changes in compilation introduced in 1986 to remove over-recording reduced the total UK count by 50,000 (Department of Employment 1990: July; see Department of Employment 1986: March/April 107–8).

–In September 1988 the changes in entitlement to benefit for those aged under 18, most of whom are now no longer eligible for Income Support, reduced the numbers by about 90,000 (Department of Employment 1990: July).

–Those on government schemes do not enter the count. During the period July 1983 to July 1989, Special Employment Measures increased by 26,000 (due to an increase of 23,000 in Youth Training Scheme and 6,000 on Employment Training). More than 400,000 16- and 17-year-olds and more than 300,000 adults are now on government schemes. This has the effect of removing a quarter of a million adults from the claimant count (Unemployment Unit and Youthaid 1989:6).

In addition to changes in counting methods there have been changes whereby those claiming benefit have been more closely screened.

–The Restart programme, introduced in July 1986 and now the main method of recruiting into temporary employment and training measures, was estimated through its interviewing procedures in 1989–90 to have the potential for removing between 11 per cent and 19 per cent from the count after allowing for those entering employment of Special Employment Measures, cutting the official unemployment count by an estimated 350,000 (Unemployment and Youthaid Unit 1989).

–More stringent screening of applicants for unemployment benefit – ensuring that entitlement to others such as invalidity benefit is taken up, so excluding them from the unemployment count – also serves to reduce official figures. *The Economist* (1989: 37) referred to these factors in trying to account for 'the disappearance from the register of three times as many men as ended up in jobs' between September 1987 and September 1988, commenting, 'so there is an increasing number of men potentially on the job market but not counted as unemployed'.

–Screening is now even more stringent since the testing of availability for work introduced in the 1989 Social Security Act. Unemployed people are now expected to demonstrate that they are 'actively seeking employment' every week.

5. Theories of labour market organization have been developed by, *inter alia*, Barron and Norris (1976); Edwards, Reich and Grodon (1975); Rubery (1980). Analysis of structural changes in the labour market associated with the recession of the 1970s in Britain can be found in Fevre (1986) and Purcell *et al.* (1986).

6. During 1984–5 there were 132,755 filled Community Programme (CP) places, with 62 per cent of entrants aged 18 to 24; a further 7,000 places on the Community Industry Scheme (CI) were filled by 17- to 19-year-olds. CP was still expanding and its intake becoming further concentrated in the 18 to 24 age group (Manpower Services Commission 1986).

7. This is not to dispute the analysis of other commentators who have drawn attention to the large numbers of older people who have become economically inactive in recent years. High levels of unemployment amongst this group are almost certainly concealed by other definitions of their status, such as sick or disabled. Bosanquet comments:

> At the extreme, in the Northern Region and in Wales, about 53 per cent of men in the 55 to 59 group and 72 per cent in the older (60 to 64) age group are effectively on the sidelines, with little or no chance of getting back into employment. In Britain as a whole the proportions are 34 per cent and 54 per cent.
>
> (Bosanquet 1987: 7–8)

8. Because the research problem made it necessary to interview young people with substantial experience of the labour market, attention was drawn to a further omission in studies of youth: the older adolescent or young adult. Some account has been taken of this age group in surveys of aspects of youth unemployment: for example, the Community Relations Commission's (1974) investigation of homelessness among white and black 18- to 25-year-olds; the survey by Roberts *et al.* (1981) of unregistered unemployment among 16- to 20-year-olds in four cities; and Ashton and Maguire's (n.d.) survey of young adults in the labour market in 1982–83 which specifically focused on 18- to 24-year-olds. Wallace's (1987) qualitative study of young people on the Isle of Sheppey includes 20-year-old men and women, as does Jenkins and Hutson's (1989) study in South Wales. Nonetheless, exceptions have mostly been confined to studies of male, often deviant, youth cultures – due largely, no doubt, to the high visibility and accessibility of such groups (see, for example, Mungham and Pearson 1976).

2 LOCAL LABOUR MARKETS AND THE HOUSEHOLD: CHANGE AND FLUX

1. In a study on the organization of work, Wilensky (1969: 127) argues that 'just as the concept of "profession" loses its precision when we speak of the "professionalization of auto workers in Detroit" so the concept of "career" loses its utility when we speak of the "career of the ditchdigger"'. A career, in this tightly conceived view, 'is a succession of related jobs, arranged in a hierarchy of prestige, through which persons move in an ordered sequence. Corollaries are that the job pattern is instituted (socially recognized and sanctioned within some social unit) and has some stability (the system is maintained over more than one generation of recruits)'(Wilensky 1969: 127).

In studies of the life course, the concept of career is used more loosely and is applied to other areas of social life. It broadly refers to changes and stages over time as the individual moves through the life course, hence the attraction of the linear associations in the term career. Brannen (1987), for example, uses the concept to disentangle the strands which make up the life course and to look at how they intersect by conceptualizing them as employment careers, domestic careers, consumption careers and motherhood careers. Whilst the stages in such careers connote progression, this may or may not follow a hierarchy of prestige. Wallace does in fact, refer to young couples 'who tend to see their futures in term of a progressional housing career involving a move every five years or so' to something better (Wallace 1987: 71). Employment careers, however, when used in the broader sense, are perhaps more accurately represented as profiles or patterns, thus encompassing increases and decreases in status. When Wilensky considered the ordered progression in the working lives of his respondents he commented, 'One fifth of the white collar workers and almost one third of the blue collar workers have gone nowhere in an unordered way'(Wilensky 1969: 128), concluding that the concept of career could not be applied to this pattern. Given these reservations, the term employment career in the Newcastle study is used in its looser form.

2. The Certificate of Secondary Education (CSE) and the General Certificate of Education (GCE) O level are now subsumed within the General Certificate of Secondary Education (GCSE).

3. Ashton and Maguire (n.d.) surveyed males and females aged between 18 and 24 in four contrasting local labour markets. They found that the character of the local labour market had greater influence upon employment chances than had personal attributes and social class. Whilst educational qualifications increased chances of obtaining work, they offered no guarantee of a job even for the highly qualified. Moreover, in areas of high unemployment such as Sunderland, where in July 1983 the unemployment rate stood at 20.1 per cent, the highly qualified were less likely to obtain work than were those with similar qualifications in the other three areas where labour markets were more buoyant. In addition, 'there was evidence that employers did not use the conventional educational qualifications as a means of discriminating between applicants' (Ashton and Maguire n.d.: 31). In fact, in Sunderland the unemployed were slightly better qualified than those in work. The authors suggest that this confirms the rationality, similar to the views expressed in the Newcastle study, that educational qualifications are no use, especially for entry into the lower end of the labour market. There was also evidence that in Sunderland, where educational achievement was lower, standards of entry into skilled work were higher than in the other three areas. This no doubt reflects the wider availability of skilled employment. It might help to explain the incremental demands for qualifications in some, lower level, jobs in Newcastle, where labour was abundant and jobs few.

4. The Manpower Services Commission (now the Training Agency), established and funded by central government, operates a range of training schemes (since 30 April 1990, contracted to the Training and Enterprise Councils) for school-leavers and young people. Many of the young people interviewed had participated in the Youth Opportunities Programme (YOP) in which placements were normally of six months duration. This had been superseded by the Youth Training Scheme (YTS), at first offering twelve-month placements and extended in

NOTES

April 1986 to a two-year programme for 16-year-olds and one year for 17-year-olds.

Although the training schemes were an important feature in the lives of all the young people, they were not a focus of the study, entering only where relevant to the particular themes which were being explored. For critical studies of the increasingly important issues of skill and vocational training see, for example, Bates *et al.* (1984); Cockburn (1987); Finn (1987); Hollands (1990).

5. A clear case where actual inside information was put to good effect was that of Martin Pearce. On learning that the colleague with whom he was currently working was about to refuse an offer of a new job with another firm, he arranged with the colleague that the letter declining the offer and Martin's letter enquiring about a job would arrive on the employer's desk by the same post.

6. The destinations of all YTS-leavers in April to January 1985, based on Manpower Services Commission survey data, and excluding those transferring to another YTS scheme, were as follows: full-time work – 58 per cent; unemployed – 30 per cent; part-time work – 4 per cent; full-time course – 4 per cent; other – 5 per cent. 'The regional figures show that the chance of a job at the end of the YTS follows almost precisely the general level of unemployment in each area . . . [I]n the Northeast, where unemployment is the worst in Britain, the proportion getting a job after the YTS is just 44 per cent . . . [L]ess than one in five in the Southeast faces the dole after their YTS, over two in five do so in the Northeast' (Lewis 1986). These figures are similar to those from the end of the Youth Opportunities Programme.

7. Ashton and Maguire report what seems to be an identical situation. They found that although those in unskilled and sales work spent less time in their first job than other groups, the evidence suggested that this 'may have more to do with the characteristics of the jobs than the characteristics of those who enter them' (Ashton and Maguire n.d.: 36). In such jobs, prospects for internal movements or promotion are poor and employees often leave because of factory closures, redundancies and the termination of short-term contracts rather than any desire to hop from job to job. As in the Newcastle study, the problem young people faced was that of securing employment. Many took a job because it was the only one available, and those who wished to move 'were prevented from doing so by the lack of opportunities and so they stuck with what they had' (Ashton and Maguire n.d.: 105).

8. Recent changes in the legal requirements governing young people's conditions of work are seen by many commentators as likely to increase the possibilities for exploitation. The Wages Act 1986 removed workers under 21 from the protection of the Wages Councils, which set rates of pay for some poorly paid jobs. Young people form about one quarter of the work-force in Wages Council Industries like shops, hotel and catering, and hairdressing. Wages Council minimum rates for young people are already low – typically between £45 and £65 per week but lower in some cases – but these minimum rates will no longer apply; nor will the young people be legally entitled to paid holidays, overtime rates or shift

169

payment (see Byrne 1986; Renn 1988). Recent employment legislation will also remove restrictions that prohibit young workers between the ages of 16 and 18 from working more than ten-and-a-half hours per day and from working night shifts and holidays (Beavis 1988).

9. Under the supplementary benefit regulations, claimants could earn up to £4 per week without any reduction in their benefit entitlement. Thereafter their benefit was reduced by an amount corresponding to the earnings less the cost of bus fares and other essentials.

10. The problem of earnings from low-paid work and entitlement to benefit is addressed in a recent pilot project jointly run by the Action Trust and the Training Agency in Sunderland, Avon and North Kent. It is a scheme whereby the Department of Social Security (DSS) allows people to take part-time temporary jobs while continuing to claim benefit. Participants' wages are saved in a personal bank account for them to cash later. It is argued that in this way people can take jobs they could not afford to take if they lost benefit, and employers can fill vacancies they would find hard to fill. It is seen as providing 'a vital stepping stone to enabling long-term unemployed people to return to work' (Meacher 1989). In the Newcastle study, whilst some of the jobs people mentioned were of the 'one-off variety', others were in the low-paid sector of the formal economy.

11. Writing of one type of career – that of middle managers and technicians in certain types of large, complex organizations – Wilensky (1969: 129) refers to 'expedient conformity (if I don't do this, I'll get into trouble)' as one of the characteristics of behaviour both at work and off work.

3 INDEPENDENCE AND WORK

1. This is not to suggest that there was a widespread, homogeneously accepted work ethic in pre-capitalist societies. For a discussion of this, see Kelvin (1984) and Rose (1985).

2. Parental behaviour is monitored by other adults. In discussing her role in the development of independence in her child, Mrs Pearce described an occasion when she responded to a question her dentist asked of her then-small son. He made the comment, 'Oh, your mother answers for you, does she?' It forced her to examine her behaviour, and following the incident she consciously restrained herself and encouraged her son to make his own responses.

3. It is recognized that some of the variability was related to gender. While important, it is not developed here.

4. Cusack and Roll (1985) have poignantly illustrated the impact of the 1984 housing benefit rules upon the relationships between parents and their teenage and young adult children who have entered the labour market. In this interview there was a hint of debt; the son said he would be able to leave home when his mother had paid her debts.

5. Ashton and Maguire (n.d.), in their study of 1,256 18-to-24-year-olds, found that 95 per cent of males and 93 per cent of females who lived in the parental home paid a contribution towards their board and lodging.

6. A 'quarter' refers to the loss of a quarter of an hour's pay for any lateness up

to fifteen minutes – even one or two minutes. This is a common practice for shop-floor workers.

7. Industrial schedules can shape family schedules, and time schedules in the public domain can also be dependent upon those in the private. Industrial schedules, for example, influence the timing of meals and of who participates; shift work, especially night work, affects the degree and quality of participation in family life. The tea-time shift which some firms adopt in order to take advantage of a specific type of female labour draws together the public schedules of the labour market and the state (through the timing of the school day) with the domestic schedule imposed on women by the imperatives of child care.

8. Morgan (1981) has noted the neglect of the role of women in the development of capitalism. This example and those in the previous note could be called the domestication of industrial time.

9. There are no official sources of information on the number of employed children under the age of 16. What evidence there is suggests that it is between a quarter and one-third of British schoolchildren. In June 1975 the Office of Population Censuses and Surveys estimated that of the 2,296,300 children aged 13, 14 and 15 in England and Wales, one-third would be workers, falling to one-quarter over ten years due to the yearly increase in this young population. In 1982–83, a survey conducted by the Low Pay Unit and the Open University found that of 1,712 children aged 11 to 16 years, interviewed in London, Luton and Bedfordshire, 40 per cent were likely to be working. Furthermore, 11- and 12-year-olds were as likely to be working during term time as the older age groups (MacLennan et al. 1985).

10. Sibling hierarchies are not necessarily simple. As well as being affected by age and employment statuses, they are also likely to be influenced by any differences in the length and type of education undergone by brothers and sisters, by gender and by courtship status.

11. This is not to say that low-paid work was always accepted because of its status as a 'proper' job.

12. Research on the role of the family in the construction of young people's economic identities is now being undertaken within the Economic and Social Research Council 16–19 Initiative's Associated Studies Programme (Allatt 1988b).

13. Wallace (1987) found that by the time they reached their early twenties, her respondents were more instrumental about the jobs they were willing to accept. 'They were instrumental in the sense that they increasingly began to think that any job was better than no job, and in the sense that a job that paid more was better than one that paid less . . . [seeing] less and less possibility of finding [job satisfaction] in the kinds of work that was available' (Wallace 1987: 128). Coffield et al. (1986) recorded the resilience of the desire for work amongst younger groups.

4 DISORDER IN TIME AND PLACE

1. The elements out of which an individual's sense of order is constructed will of course be influenced by such structural and cultural variables as

class, ethnicity and gender. The purpose of the analysis, however, was not to pursue these differences but rather to set out some of the ways in which we can think about the issues.

2. Although in the literature and in the comments of the people interviewed marriage symbolized full adulthood and 'settling down', some of the young women rejected the idea of marriage, noting, for example, how it had changed the lives of their older sisters. The responses of young women in Wallace's (1987) study echoed this sentiment; a few years later, nonetheless, the respondents were married.

3. The connection between unemployment, the resulting drop in income, and ill health is one of debate. Carr-Hill (1987) argues that the claim that unemployment *per se* has effects on physical health is rarely evidenced. Platt, however, notes studies which he claims 'point unequivocally to a deterioration in psychological health caused by unemployment' (Platt 1986: 151).

4. Wallace (1987) records similar parental comments in her study.

5. The incidence of illegitimate births rose from 9 per cent in 1970 to 23 per cent in 1987. Many of them were registered by both parents – 68 per cent in 1987, of whom 70 per cent were living at the same address (*The Guardian* 1989, 6 Sept.). According to the 1988 General Household Survey, 21 per cent of single women were cohabiting (*The Guardian* 1989, 6 Dec.).

6. Ronald Frankenberg pointed out this connection when the paper on which this chapter is based was read at the Annual Conference of the Association for Social Studies of Time, Dartington, 1987.

5 THE MORAL COMMUNITY

1. Despite the diversity in our society, major elements of a common culture are shared. From the viewpoint of an historian, E. P. Thompson has interpreted cultural variation not as 'segregated and antithetical . . . cultures but rather a plurality of emphasis (class, racial, gender or occupational) within a unitary sum (Thompson 1984: 161). Similar conclusions emerged in a sociological analysis of family ideology in documentary sources: components of a shared ideology were differently articulated according to the source of information and the class, gender and marital status of the audience (Allatt 1981b).

2. The traditional family structure of Italian families transplanted to the modern industrial environment of Buffalo over the period 1900 to 1930 was maintained by the selective utilization of the employment opportunities open to women so as to conform to the obtaining cultural pattern. Male dominance showed in the occupational style of the women whose economic activity was either confined to the home – for example in servicing lodgers – or undertaken in the company of relatives in the seasonal canning and harvesting occupations even when better economic opportunities were available (McLoughlin 1973: 12).

3. After discussing the classification in tribal societies and certain categorizations of individuals as a mechanism of social control, Douglas turns to an examination of our own:

In another type of society the probability of being accused of pollution will fall on paupers and second-class citizens of various types. Paupers I define as those who, by falling below a required level of achievement, are not able to enter into exchanges of gifts, services and hospitality. They find themselves not only excluded from the main responsibilities and pleasures of citizenship but a charge upon the community. They are a source of embarrassment to their more prosperous fellows and a living contradiction to any current theories about the equality of man.

(Douglas 1975: 240)

Representations of 'the poor' as a polluting 'underclass' whose values are contaminating the life of entire neighbourhoods in British society have recently achieved some prominence (Murray 1989).
4. In her study of women's leisure, Deem writes, 'Both working- and middle-class girls face similar problems of male control over what they can or cannot do. As girls grow older the agent of that control may shift from fathers to boyfriends' (Deem 1987: 109).
5. Ashton and Maguire (n.d.) found that word of mouth was the most frequently used method of obtaining first jobs in the North-East, as elsewhere, with the exception of St Alban's (representing the more affluent southern regions) and for the higher occupational levels. For subsequent jobs, word of mouth as a method of finding a job increased, suggesting the importance of being in work in order to gain access to information

APPENDIX 2

1. A visit to a local church and its graveyard provided some historical evidence of the earlier dominance of work in the lives of people living in this neighbourhood. This dominance was literally carved in metal and stone. A large brass plaque fixed to one of the inner walls of the church distinguished workers from the rest of the community, reading:

The tablet was erected by the workmen and inhabitants of 'Eldon' Wallsend and district in appreciation of the patriotism shewn by the Service Company of the Second Volunteer Battalion Northumberland Fusiliers in response to the Nation's call to assist in the suppression of the Boer insurrection in South Africa 1900–1901 1902.

In the graveyard, gravestones dating from 1848 to 1929 carried inscriptions which referred to the occupation, occupational status and place of work of the deceased. Some had been erected through voluntary subscription by subordinates, some by fellow members of, for example, the local branch of the Boiler Makers and Iron Ship Builders' Society, some by family members; others were not specific. For example, one from 1880 marks 'The burial place of John Matthews of 'Eldon' Iron Works and Margaret his wife'. Such identifiers are not confined to the workers in heavy industry; a farmer's wife is commemorated in 1852 and a surgeon in 1875. Some of the inscriptions also refer to deaths arising from accidents in the local pits and shipyards.

Such practices may have been common. Ian Keil, economic historian, notes a study which does not refer to gravestones but which emphasizes the importance of work and respect from fellow workers at the burial (personal communication). The chance discovery of these inscriptions can only hint at Eldon's past. It does, however, provide some evidence to support the distinct reputation which Eldon held, or had held, in the eyes of local people.

BIBLIOGRAPHY

Allan, G. A. (1982) 'Property and family solidarity', in P.G. Hollowell (ed.) *Property and Social Relations*, London: Heinemann.

Allatt, P. (1981a) 'Stereotyping: Familism in the law', in B. Fryer, A. Hunt, D. McBarnet and B. Moorhouse (eds) *Law, State and Society*, London: Croom Helm.

——(198lb) 'The family seen through the Beveridge Report, forces' education and popular magazines: a sociological study of the social reproduction of family ideology in World War II', unpublished Ph.D. thesis, University of Keele.

——(1986a) 'The young unemployed: Independence and identity', in B. Pashley (ed.) *Youth Unemployment and the Transition to Adulthood*, Papers in Social Policy and Professional Studies No. 4, Department of Social policy and Professional Studies, Hull: University of Hull.

——(1986b) 'The dis-ease of social change: Time in the lives of young people and their parents in time and place of mass unemployment', paper given at the Association for Social Studies of Time Annual Conference, Dartington, July.

——(1987) 'In trust: young people and transfers within households', paper given at ESRC Workshop Resources within Households, Institute of Education, University of London.

——(1988a) 'Time to leave?', *New Society* 83 (1 April): 19–21.

——(1988b) 'Family processes and transfers in the transition to adulthood', ESRC 16–19 Initiative, Associated Study, ESRC grant no. XC05250019.

——(1990) *A Cultural Comparison of Young People and Their Families in Times of Social and Economic Change: The Case of Britain and Spain* (work in progress, British Council).

Allatt, P. and Yeandle, S.M. (1986) '"It's not fair, is it?" Youth unemployment, family relations and the social contract', in S. Allen, K. Purcell, A. Watson and S. Wood (eds) *The Experience of Unemployment*, London: Macmillan.

Anderson, M. (1971) *Family Structure in Nineteenth Century Lancashire*, Cambridge: Cambridge University Press.

Ashton, D. and Maguire, M.J. (n.d.) *Young Adults in the Labour Market*, Department of Employment Research Paper No. 55, London: Department of Employment.

Backett, K. (1982) *Mothers and Fathers*, New York: St. Martin's Press.

Baier, A.C. (1985) 'What do women want in a moral philosophy?', *Nous* XIX, No. 1: 53–63.

Banfield, E.C. (1958) *The Moral Basis of a Backward Society*, New York: The Free Press.

Banks, M.H. and Jackson, P.R. (1982) 'Unemployment and risk of minor psychiatric disorder in young people: Cross-sectional and longitudinal evidence', *Psychological Medicine* 12: 789–98.

Barron, R.D. and Norris, G.H. (1976) 'Sexual divisions in the dual labour market', in D.L. Barker and S. Allen (eds) *Dependence and Exploitation in Work and Marriage*, London: Longman.

Bates, I. (n.d.a) 'No bleeding, whining minnies: The role of YTS in class and gender reproductions', *ESRC 16–19 Initiative Occasional Papers* (No. 19), London: Social Statistics Research Unit, City University.

——(n.d.b) 'Designer careers. An analysis focussing on the influence of family background, gender and the vocational track on female careers', *ESRC 16–19 Initiative Occasional Papers* (No. 23), London: Social Statistics Research Unit, City University.

Bates, I., Clarke, J., Cohen, P., Finn, D., Moore, R. and Whillis, P. (1984) *Schooling for the Dole? The New Vocationalism*, London: Macmillan.

Beavis, S. (1988) 'Fowler ends "dated" hours limit for young', *Guardian* 2 Dec.

Becker, H.S. (1986) *Writing for Social Scientists: How to Start and Finish Your Thesis, Book, or Article*, Chicago: Chicago University Press.

Bell, C. and McKee, L. (1982) *Marital and Family Relations in Times of Male Unemployment*, Department of Sociology and Social History, University of Aston, ESRC grant no. G0023004.

Blau, P. (1964) *Exchange and Power in Social Life*, New York: Wiley.

Bosanquet, N. (1987) *A Generation in Limbo: Government, the Economy and the 55–65 Age Group in Britain*, London: Public Policy Centre.

Bourdieu, P. (1971) 'Reproduction culturelle et reproduction sociale', *Information sur les Sciences Sociales* (Social Science Information) 10, (2) (cited in Nowotny 1981).

Bradshaw, J., Lawton, D., and Cook, E.E. (1987) 'Income, expenditure and teenagers and their families', *Youth and Policy* 19: 15–19.

Brannen, J. (1987) 'The resumption of employment after childbirth: A turning point within a life course perspective', in P. Allatt, T. Keil, A. Bryman and B. Bytheway (eds) *Women and the Life Cycle: Transitions and Turning Points*, London: Macmillan.

Breakwell, G. (1984) 'Knowing your place: Finding your place again', *ESRC Newsletter* 52: 29–30, London: Economic and Social Research Council.

Brelsford, P., Smith, G. and Rix, A. (1982) *Give Us a Break: Widening Opportunities for Young Women within YOP/YTS*, Manpower Services Commission Research and Development Series No. 11, Sheffield: Manpower Services Commission, Training Division.

Brock, P. (1985) 'Why the unemployed are getting the blame being jobless', *The Guardian* 1 May.

Brown, L.H. and Kidwell, J.S. (1982) 'Methodology in family studies: The other side of caring', *Journal of Marriage and the Family* 44 (November): 833–39.

Bulmer, M. (1986) *Neighbours: The Work of Philip Abrams*, Cambridge: Cambridge University Press.

Burgoyne, J. (1983) 'Accounts and reality', paper presented at workshop: *Problems of Methodology in Family/Household Research*, University of Aston, 20 May.

Byrne, D. (1986) 'Back to the sweatshop', *Youthaid*, 28 (Sept./Oct.): 9.

Campbell, D.T. and Stanley, J.C. (1963) *Experimental and Quasi-Experimental Designs for Research*, Chicago: Rand McNally.

Carmichael, K. (1986) 'Saints and sinners', *New Society* 75 (7 February): 233.

Carr, S. (1984) *Changing Patterns of Work*, London: Workers Educational Association.

Carr-Hill, R. (1987) 'The inequalities in health debate: A critical review of the issues', *Journal of Social Policy* 16: 509–53.

Carroll, P. (1979) *The Social and Psychological Effects of Unemployment Upon Young People – A Review of the Literature*, London: Department of Employment (unpublished).

Central Statistical Office (1984) *Social Trends*, London: CSO.

Chaney, J. (1985) 'Returning to work', in P. Close and R. Collins (eds) *Family and Economy in Modern Society*, London: Macmillan.

City of Newcastle upon Tyne (1981a) 'Report of the Director Housing', October (unpublished).

——(1981b) 'High unemployment in the inner city', Newcastle upon Tyne: Policy Service Unit.

Cockburn, C. (1987) *Two Track Training. Sex Inequalities and the YTS*, London: Macmillan.

Coffield, F.J., Borrill, C. and Marshall, S. (1983) 'How young people try to survive being unemployed', *New Society* 64: 332–34.

Coffield, F., Borrill, C. and Marshall, S. (1986) *Growing Up at the Margins: Young People in the North East*, Milton Keynes: Open University Press.

Community Relations Commission (1974) *Unemployed and Homeless: A Report*, London: Her Majesty's Stationery Office.

Conger, J.J. (1973) *Adolescence and Youth*, New York: Harper International Edition.

Cooke, P. (ed.) (1986) *Global Restructing Local Response. A Report Commissioned by the Environment and Planning Committee of the ESRC*, London: Economic and Social Research Council.

Corrigan, P. (1989) 'Gender and the gift: The case of the family clothing economy', *Sociology* 23: 513–36.

Counter Information Services (1976) 'The cuts hit home', in *Crisis: Women under Attack*, Anti-Report 15, London: Counter Information Services.

Cousins, J. (1980) *Employment in the Inner City – Attitudes, Aspirations and Opportunities*, First Report: Households. Individuals and the Economically Active in Three Areas of Newcastle upon Tyne. Second Report: Characteristics and Attitudes in the Economically Active in Three Areas of Newcastle upon Tyne, Durham: Department of Sociology and Social Policy, University of Durham.

Cusack, S. and Roll, J. (1985) *Families Rent Apart: A Study of Young People's Contributions to Their Parents' Housing Costs*, London: Child Poverty Action Group and Youthaid.

Daniel, W.W. (1981) *The Unemployed Flow, Stage 1, Interim Report*, London: Policy Studies Institute.

Deem, R. (1987) '"My husband says I'm too old for dancing": Women, leisure and life cycles', in P. Allatt, T. Keil, A. Bryman and B. Bytheway (eds) *Women and the Life Cycle: Transitions and Turning Points*, London: Macmillan.

Department of Education and Science (1983) *Young People in the 80s: A Survey*, London: Her Majesty's Stationery Office.

Department of Employment (1984) *Employment Gazette* (February, September, December) London: Her Majesty's Stationery Office.

——(1986) *Employment Gazette* (March/April), London: Her Majesty's Stationery Office.

——(1990) *Employment Gazette* (June), London: Her Majesty's Stationery Office.

Douglas, M. (1966) *Purity and Danger: An Analysis of the Concepts of Pollution and Taboo*, London: Routledge & Kegan Paul.

——(1975) *Implicit Meanings: Essays in Anthropology*, London: Routledge & Kegan Paul.

Durkheim, E. (1957) *Professional Ethics and Civic Morals*, Cornelia Brookfield (trans.), London: Routledge & Kegan Paul.

Economist, The (1988) 'Economic and financial indicators: Jobs', 309 (7575, 5 November): 167.

——(1989) 'Unemployment: Past the milestone', 310 (7590, 18 February): 37.

Edwards, R., Reich, M., and Grodon, D. (1975) *Labor Market Segmentation*, Lexington, Mass.: D.C. Heath.

Elder, G.H. (1978) 'Family history and the life course', in T.K. Hareven (ed.) *Transitions: The Family and the Life Course in Historical Perspective*, New York: Academic Press.

Elias, N. and Scotson, J.L. (1965) *The Established and the Outsiders*, London: Frank Cass.

Elliott, L. (1989) 'Chronic jobless cut by 50pc', *The Guardian* 23 August.

Fagin, L. and Little, M. (1984) *The Forsaken Families*, Harmondsworth: Penguin.

Fevre, R. (1986) 'Contract work and the recession', in K. Purcell, S. Wood, A. Watson and S. Allen (eds) *The Changing Experience of Employment: Restructuring and Recession*, London: Macmillan.

Finn, D. (1987) *Training without Jobs: New Deals and Broken Promises*, London: Macmillan.

Fitz, J. and Hood-Williams, J. (1981) 'The generation game', in D. Robbins (ed.) *Rethinking Social Inequality*, Explorations in Sociology 15, Aldershot: Gower.

Frankenberg, R.J. (ed) (forthcoming) *Time and Health*, London: Sage.

Freedman, M. (1969) *The Process of Work Establishment*, New York: Columbia University Press.

Glaser, B.L., and Strauss, A.L. (1967) *The Discovery of Grounded Theory*, London: Weidenfeld & Nicholson.

Goffman, E. (1968) *Asylums: Essays on the Social Situation of Mental Patients and Other Inmates*, Harmondsworth: Penguin.

Gouldner, A.W. (1960) 'The norm of reciprocity: A preliminary statement,' *American Sociological Review* 25 (2): 161–78.

Green, D. (1981) *Power and Party in an English City: An Account of Single-Party Rule*, London: George Allen and Unwin.

Griffin, C. (1985) *Typical Girls? Young women from School to the Job Market*, London: Routledge & Kegan Paul.

——(1987) 'Broken transitions: From school to the scrap heap' in P. Allatt, T. Keil, A. Bryman and B. Bytheway (eds) *Women and the Life Cycle: Transitions and Turning Points*, London: Macmillan.

Guardian, The (1982) *The Guardian*, 8 March.

Hakim, c. (1979) *Occupational Segregation: A Comparative Study of the Degree and Pattern of the Differentiation Between Men's and Women's Work in Britain, the United States and Other Countries*, Research Paper No. 9, London: Department of Employment.

Hareven, T.K. (1982) *Family Time and Industrial Time: The Relationship Between the Family and Work in a New England Industrial Community*, Cambridge: Cambridge University Press.

Harris, C.C. (1985) ESCR Workshop on Ageing.

Harris, N. (1988) 'Social security and the transition to adulthood', *Journal of Social Policy* 17: 501–23.

Hollands, R. (1990) *The Long Transition: Class, Culture and Youth Training*, London: Macmillan.

Holley. J.C. (1981) 'The two family economies of industrialism: Factory workers in Victorian Scotland', *Journal of Family History* 6 (1): 57–69.

Husbands, C.T. (1985) 'Government popularity and the unemployment issue, 1966–1983', *Sociology* 19: 1–18.

Hutson, J. and Jenkins, R. (1987) 'Family Relationships and the Unemployment of Young People in South Wales', in Michael White (ed.) *The Social World of the Young Unemployed*, London: Policy Studies Institute.

——(1989) *Taking the Strain: Family, Unemployment and the Transition to Adulthood*, Buckingham: Open University Press.

Jahoda, M., Lazarsfeld, P.F. and Zeisel, H. (1972) *Marienthal: The Sociography of an Unemployed Community* (first published 1933), London: Tavistock.

Jenkins, R., Bryman, A., Ford, J., Keil, T. and Beardsworth, A. (1983) 'Information in the labour market: The impact of recession', *Sociology* 17: 260–67.

Kelvin, P. (1984) 'The historical dimension of social psychology: The case of unemployment', in H. Tajfel (ed.) *The Social Dimension Vol. 2*, Cambridge: Cambridge University Press.

Kelvin, P. and Jarrett, J. (1985) *Unemployment, its Social and Psychological Effects*, Cambridge: Cambridge University Press.

Kiernan, K.E. (1985) 'Leaving Home: questions and queries from statistics,' paper presented at Workshop 5: Problems in Methodology in

Family Household Research, University of Manchester, Manchester, 22 November.

Komarovsky, M. (1962) *Blue Collar Marriage*, New York: Random House.

——(1971) *The Unemployed Man and His Family: The Effects of Unemployment on the Status of the Man in 59 Families* (first published 1940), New York: Octagon Books.

Kornhauser, W. (1960) *The Politics of Mass Society*, London: Routledge & Kegan Paul.

Lakoff, G. and Johnson, M. (1981) 'Conceptual metaphor in everyday language', in M. Johnson (ed.) *Philosophical Perspectives on Metaphor*, Minneapolis: University of Minneapolis Press.

Lampedusa, Giuseppe Tomasi di (1988) *The Leopard* (first published 1958) Glasgow: Collins.

Land, (1979) 'Boundaries between the state and the family', in C.C. Harris (ed.), *The Sociology of the Family: New Directions in Britain*, Sociological Review Monograph 28, Keele: University of Keele.

Leiulfsrud, H. and Woodward, A. (1987) 'Women at class crossroads', *Sociology* 21: 393–414.

Leonard, D. (1980) *Sex and Generation: A Study of Courtship and Weddings*, London: Tavistock.

Lewis, P. (1985) 'Introduction: Policies towards young people' in Cusack, S. and Roll, J., *Families Rent Apart: A Study of Young People's Contributions to their Parents' Housing Costs*, London: Child Poverty Action Group and Youthaid.

——(1986) 'YTS leavers', *Youthaid Bulletin* 29 (November/December): 4–5, 12.

——(1987) 'Lord Young's flexible friends', *Youthaid Bulletin* 30 (January/February): 6–8.

Lister, R. and Wilson, L. (1976) *The Unequal Breadwinner. A New Perspective on Women and Social Security*, London: National Council for Civil Liberties.

Littler, C.R. (ed.) (1985) *The Experience of Work*, Aldershot: Gower (in association with the Open University).

Longfield, J. (1984) *Ask the Family: Shattering Myths about Family Life*, London: Bedford Square Press/National Council for Voluntary Organisation.

McKee, L. and Bell, C. (1986) 'His unemployment, her problem: The domestic and the marital consequences of male unemployment', in (eds) S. Allen, K. Purcell, Watson B. and S. Wood, *The Experience of Unemployment*, London: Macmillan.

MacLennan, E., Fitz, J. and Sullivan, J. (1985) *Working Children*, Low Pay Pamphlet No. 34, London: Low Pay Unit.

McLoughlin, V.Y. (1973) 'Patterns of work and family organization: Buffalo Italians', in T.K. Rabb and R.I. Rotberg (eds) *The Family in History: Interdisciplinary Essays*, New York: Harper and Row.

Manpower Services Commission (1986) *Annual Report 1985/86*, Sheffield: Manpower Services Commission.

Marsden, D. (1982) *Workless: An Exploration of the Social Contract Between Society and the Worker*, revised edn., London: Croom Helm.

Mauss, M. (1954) *The Gift: Forms and Functions of Exchange in Archaic Societies*, London: Cohen and West.

Meacher, M. (1989) 'A brave step for the long-term unemployed', letter to *The Guardian*, 13 Sept.

Metcalf, D. (1982) 'Goodbye steel and cars and planes', *New Society* 59 (21 January): 91–3.

Mills, C.W. (1959) *The Sociological Imagination*, Oxford: Oxford University Press.

Molotoch, H. (1975) 'Power', Presentation to the Department of Sociology and Social Anthropology, University of Keele.

Moore, B., Jr (1978) *Injustice: The Social Basis of Obedience and Revolt*, New York: M.E. Sharpe.

Morgan, A.E. (1939) *The Needs of Youth. A Report Made to King George's Jubilee Trust Fund*, London: Oxford University Press.

Morgan, D.H.J. (1975) *Social Theory and the Family*, London: Routledge & Kegan Paul.

——(1977) 'Alternatives to the family', in R. Chester and J. Peel (eds) *Equalities and Inequalities in Family Life*, London: Academic Press.

——(1981) 'Men, masculinity and the process of sociological enquiry', in H. Roberts (ed.) *Doing Feminist Research*, London: Routledge & Kegan Paul.

——(1985) *The Family, Politics and Social Theory*, London: Routledge & Kegan Paul.

Morris, L.D. (1986) 'The changing social structure of Hartlepool', in P. Cooke (ed.) *Global Restructuring Local Response*. A Report Commissioned by the Environment and Planning Committee of the ESRC, London: Economic and Social Research Council.

Mungham, G. and Pearson, G. (eds) (1976) *Working Class Youth Culture*, London: Routledge & Kegan Paul.

Murcott, A. (1983) '"It's a pleasure to cook for him": Food, mealtimes and gender in South Wales households', in E. Gamarnikow, D. Morgan, J. Purvis and D. Taylorson (eds.) *The Public and the Private*, London: Heinemann.

Murray, C. (1989) 'Underclass: A disaster in the making', *Sunday Times Magazine*, 26 November: 26–46.

National Economic Development Council (n.d.) *Changing Patterns of Work: How Companies Introduce Flexibility to Meet New Needs*, London: National Economic Development Council.

New Society (1985) 'Losing control over life', *New Society* 74 (18 October): 112.

North Tyneside Community Development Project (CDP) (1978) *North Shields: Living with Industrial Change*. Final Report Vol. 2, Newcastle upon Tyne: Newcastle upon Tyne Polytechnic.

Nowotny, H. (1981) 'Women in Public Life in Austria', in C. Fuchs Epstein and R. Laub Coser (eds) *Access to Power: Cross National Studies of Women and Elites*, London: George Allen and Unwin.

Pahl, J. (1983) 'The allocation of money and the structuring of inequality within marriage', *Sociological Review* 31: 237–62.

Pahl, R.E. (1984) *Divisions of Labour*, London: Basil Blackwell.

181

Parkes, C.M (1984) 'Foreword', in Fagin, L. and Little, M. *The Forsaken Families*, Harmondsworth: Penguin.

Parsons, T. and Bales, F.R. (1956) *Family, Socialization and Interaction Process*, London: Routledge & Kegan Paul.

Phillips, D. (1973) 'Young and unemployed in a Northern city', in D. Weir (ed.) *Men and Work in Modern Britain*, London: Fontana.

Pilgrim Trust, The (1938) *Men Without Work. A Report Made to the Pilgrim Trust*, Cambridge: Cambridge University Press.

Piotrkowski, M. (1979) *Work and the Family System*, New York: The Free Press.

Platt, S. (1986) 'Recent trends in parasuicide ("attempted suicide") and unemployment amongst men in Edinburgh', in S. Allen, K. Purcell, A. Watson and S. Wood (eds) *The Experience of Unemployment*, London: Macmillan.

Purcell, K., Wood, S., Watson, A., and Allen, S. (1986) *The Changing Experience of Unemployment: Restructuring and Recession*, London: Macmillan.

Raffe, D. (1986) 'Change and continuity in the youth labour market: a critical review of structural explanations of youth unemployment', in S. Allen, A. Watson, K. Purcell and S. Wood (eds), *The Experience of Unemployment*, London: Macmillan.

Rathkey, P. (n.d.) *Youth Unemployment in Cleveland*, Cleveland: Cleveland Conway Memorial Foundation.

Rees, T. (1983) 'Boys off the street and girls in the home: Youth unemployment and state intervention in Northern Ireland', in R. Fidday (ed.) *In Place of Work*, Lewes: The Falmer Press.

Renn, M. (1988) 'The lady who plays stopper for the youth team', *The Guardian*, 12 Oct.

Rimmer, L. (n.d.) *Unemployment and the Family: The Social and Economic Effects of Unemployment*, Working Paper No. 4, London: Study Commission on the family.

Roberts, K., Duggan, J. and Noble, M. (1981) *Unregistered Youth Unemployment and Outreach Careers Work: Final Report, Part One: Non-Registration*. Department of Employment Research Paper 31, London: Department of Employment.

Rose, M. (1985) *Reworking the Work Ethic: Economic Values of Socio-Cultural Politics*, London: Batsford.

Rubery, J. (1980) 'Structured labour markets, worker organisation and low pay', in A.H. Amsden (ed.) *The Economics of Women and Work*, Harmondsworth: Penguin.

Salmon, P. (1985) *Living in Time: A New Look at Personal Development*, London: Dent.

Schofield, M. (1965) *The Sexual Behaviour of Young People*, London: Longman.

Selbourne, D. (1982) 'Wolverhampton on ice', *New Society* 59 (21 January): 94–6.

Spence, M. (1985) 'Nice work if you can get it', *New Statesman* 109 (22 February): 8–9.

Stacey, M. (1969) *Methods of Social Research*, Oxford: Pergamon Press.

Taylor, R. (1982) 'Young hardcore', *New Society* 59 (25 February): 308–9.

Thompson, E.P. (1984) 'The image and reality of war', *New Society* 69 (23 August): 159–61.

Tyne and Wear County-Wide Research and Intelligence Unit (1986) *Unemployment in Tyne and Wear*, Newcastle: Newcastle Civic Centre, April.

—— (1990) Tyne and Wear Statistics (unpublished).

Ullah, P. (1987) 'Unemployed black youths in a Northern city', in D. Fryer and P. Ullah (eds) *Unemployed People: Social and Psychological Perspectives*, Milton Keynes: Open University Press.

Unemployment Unit and Youthaid (1989) *Working Brief: Analysis of Current Training and Employment Issues and Monthly Labour Market Statistics* (October), London: Unemployment Unit and Youthaid.

Wallace, C. (1987) *For Richer for Poorer. Growing Up In and Out of Work*, London: Tavistock.

Wallman, S. (1984) *Eight London Households*, London: Tavistock.

White, M. (1983) *Long-Term Unemployment and Labour Markets*, London: Policy Studies Institute.

Wilensky, H.L. (1969) 'Work, careers and social integration', in T. Burns (ed.) *Industrial Man: Selected Readings*, Harmondsworth: Penguin. (First published 1960, *International Social Science Journal* 12: 543–74.)

Yeandle, S. (1984) *Women's Working Lives: Patterns and Strategies*, London: Tavistock.

Youthaid (1986a) 'The Social Security Bill', *Youthaid Bulletin* 25 (March): 4–5.

——(1986b) 'Young jam for old', *Youthaid Bulletin* 27 (July/August): 1.

Zerubavel, E. (1981) *Hidden Rhythms: Schedules and Calendars in Social Life*, Berkeley, California: University of California Press.

INDEX OF INFORMANTS

NAME INDEX

186

SUBJECT INDEX